PRAYER STORM
DAILY PRAYER GUIDE

ENLARGED THROUGH INTIMACY & FAITH

JANUARY – FEBRUARY 2026

Godson T. Nembo

ENLARGED THROUGH INTIMACY & FAITH

Copyright @ December 2025

Published in Cameroon by:
Christian Restoration Network
crnprayerstorm@gmail.com,
prayerstorm@christianrestorationnetwork.org

ISBN: 978-1-63603-364-8

All rights reserved!
No portion of this book may be used without the written permission of the publisher, with the exception of brief excerpts in magazines, articles reviews, etc.
All scripture quotations are from the New King James Version (NKJV) of the Bible except otherwise stated.

CONTACT
P.O. Box 31339 Biyem-assi, Yaounde, Cameroon
Tel.: 679.46.57.17, 652.38.26.93 or 696.56.58.64
Email: **godsonnembo@gmail.com** or
contact@christianrestorationnetwork.org
www.christianrestorationnetwork.org

WHERE TO BUY THIS PRAYER GUIDE:
SEE THE LAST PAGE

YOU CAN ACCESS ALL PRINTED HARD COPIES

OF OUR BOOKS FOR ANY SPECIFIED DURATION AT YOUR DOORSTEP.
Contact (237) 679465717 for subscription and payment details.

Prayer Storm Online Store: With MTN or Orange Mobile Money *(for those in Cameroon)* and E-Wallet *(for those abroad)*, you can easily obtain the electronic version of this book and other CRN publications via **www.amazon.com** at **https://shorturl.at/pqxyT** or **www.christianrestorationnetwork.org/our-bookstore** or **https://goo.gl/ktf3rT**

Printed in Yaounde, Cameroon by Mama press: (237) 677581523

TESTIMONIES:
Your testimony is a weapon against the kingdom of darkness. It is also a seed for someone else's miracle. Share with us what God has used this prayer guide and our books to do in your life; by SMS, telephone call or email.

BECOME A MINISTRY PARTNER:
Call the numbers: (237) 679.46.57.17 or 652.38.26.93 or 696.56.58.64 or send an email to:
crnprayerstorm@gmail.com or
contact@christianrestorationnetwork.org

Send your financial seed to:
- ECOBANK Acc. N°: **0040812604565101**

- Carmel Cooperative Credit Union Ltd. Bamenda Acc. Nº: **261**
- ORANGE Mobile Money Acc. Nº: **699902618**
- MTN Mobile Money Acc. Nº: **674495895**

A NEED FOR DISTRIBUTORS:

If you are interested in the distribution of this Prayer Storm Daily Prayer Guide, call or send an SMS to any of these numbers for negotiations: (237) 675.68.60.05 or 677.43.69.64 or 652.38.26.93 or 696.56.58.64 or send an email to: **crnprayerstorm@gmail.com** (see last page).

TABLE OF CONTENTS

IMPORTANT EVENTS/ANNOUNCEMENTS ... X

HOW TO BECOME A CHILD OF GOD XIII

NOW THAT YOU ARE BORN AGAIN XV

HOW TO USE THIS DAILY PRAYER GUIDE
.... XVIII

THURSDAY 1 JANUARY	THE FOUNDATION FOR ENLARGEMENT .. 21
FRIDAY 2 JANUARY	ENLARGED IN THE SECRET PLACE 24
SATURDAY 3 JANUARY	LENGTHEN THE CORD OF PRAYER 26
SUNDAY 4 JANUARY	THE CALL TO ABIDE 28
MONDAY 5 JANUARY	ENLARGED THROUGH OBEDIENCE 41
TUESDAY 6 JANUARY	LET THE HOLY SPIRIT INCUBATE YOU 44
WEDNESDAY 7 JANUARY	FOCUS ON DIVINE DIRECTION 46
THURSDAY 8 JANUARY	THE SINS OF SODOM 48

FRIDAY 9 JANUARY	ACTIVATE YOUR SPIRITUAL SENSES 50
SATURDAY 10 JANUARY	TRAPPED BY FASTING? 52
SUNDAY 11 JANUARY	THE POWER OF VISION 54
MONDAY 12 JANUARY	STAY WITH THE HOLY SPIRIT 57
TUESDAY 13 JANUARY	UNLOCKING THE TREASURES OF DARKNESS 60
WEDNESDAY 14 JANUARY	BE A MAN OR WOMAN OF PEACE 62
THURSDAY 15 JANUARY	PUT YOUR LIFE IN ORDER 64
FRIDAY 16 JANUARY	RESPONDING TO DIVINE REVELATION 66
SATURDAY 17 JANUARY	DO NOT SPARE! . 68
SUNDAY 18 JANUARY	WHEN GOD WANTS TO DESTROY A MAN 70
MONDAY 19 JANUARY	ENLARGED THROUGH SUFFERING 72
TUESDAY 20 JANUARY	ENLARGED

	THROUGH BROKENNESS 75
WEDNESDAY 21 JANUARY	SEEK HIS FACE, NOT JUST HIS HAND 78
THURSDAY 22 JANUARY	FORGET THE SHAMEFUL PAST 80
FRIDAY 23 JANUARY	WASHED IN MILK 83
SATURDAY 24 JANUARY	PERFUMED WITH MYRRH 85
SUNDAY 25 JANUARY	DESTROY THE VEIL OF PRIDE ... 87
MONDAY 26 JANUARY	DON'T EAT YOUR SEED 89
TUESDAY 27 JANUARY	SEVEN LAWS OF MAKING MONEY 92
WEDNESDAY 28 JANUARY	FIVE WAYS TO START A PETIT BUSINESS 95
THURSDAY 29 JANUARY	ACCELERATING IN FAVOUR 98
FRIDAY 30 JANUARY	ENJOYING SPIRITUAL IMMUNITY 100
SATURDAY 31 JANUARY	VALUE COVENANT

	RELATIONSHIPS 102
SUNDAY 1 FEBRUARY	CROSS INTO THE REALM OF FAITH 104
MONDAY 2 FEBRUARY	FAITH THAT OPENS THE IMPOSSIBLE 106
TUESDAY 3 FEBRUARY	FAITH THAT OPENS DOORS ..109
WEDNESDAY 4 FEBRUARY	ASK GOD FOR A STRATEGY 111
THURSDAY 5 FEBRUARY	WHAT IS DRIVING YOU? 113
FRIDAY 6 FEBRUARY	THE GOD WHO DEFENDS YOUR PORTION.............115
SATURDAY 7 FEBRUARY	RUN TO THE CITY OF REFUGE........117
SUNDAY 8 FEBRUARY	JESUS CHRIST YOUR HUSBAND 119
MONDAY 9 FEBRUARY	GOD'S WISDOM FOR BUSINESS GROWTH............121
TUESDAY 10 FEBRUARY	BE THE CHANGE YOU WANT TO SEE......................123

WEDNESDAY 11 FEBRUARY	A BLESSED CITIZEN	125
THURSDAY 12 FEBRUARY	STAND YOUR GROUND	127
FRIDAY 13 FEBRUARY	PRIORITIZE THE ESSENTIALS	129
SATURDAY 14 FEBRUARY	MAKE YOUR MARRIAGE HONORABLE	131
SUNDAY 15 FEBRUARY	WHAT IS EATING YOU UP?	133
MONDAY 16 FEBRUARY	PEACE IN THE STORM	135
TUESDAY 17 FEBRUARY	KEEP YOUR CONSCIENCE PURE	138
WEDNESDAY 18 FEBRUARY	HOW NOT TO FADE AWAY	141
THURSDAY 19 FEBRUARY	GOD TAKES TIME TO DO CERTAIN THINGS	143
FRIDAY 20 FEBRUARY	THE BEST PRAYER	145
SATURDAY 21 FEBRUARY	ROOT IT OUT!	147
SUNDAY 22 FEBRUARY	PEACE BE WITH YOU	149
MONDAY 23 FEBRUARY	PURIFIED BY GOD	151

TUESDAY 24 FEBRUARY	IS SOMEONE TRYING TO BRING YOU DOWN?......**154**
WEDNESDAY 25 FEBRUARY	YOUR NAME SHOULD NOT STOP YOU **156**
THURSDAY 26 FEBRUARY	SOURCE OF FAMILY STRENGTH.........**158**
FRIDAY 27 FEBRUARY	HE WILL CARRY YOU......................**161**
SATURDAY 28 FEBRUARY	FAILURE IS NOT AN OPTION........**163**

WHAT YOUR SUPPORT WILL DO 165

TESTIMONY 165

WHERE TO BUY THIS PRAYER GUIDE...........166

PUBLICATIONS BY CHRISTIAN RESTORATION NETWORK (CRN/PRAYER STORM).............172

x

IMPORTANT EVENTS/ANNOUNCEMENTS

SPECIAL PRAYER STORM PROGRAM			
21 DAYS FASTING AND PRAYER TO TAKE OVER THE NEW YEAR	Theme	Date	Venue
	ENLARGED BY GOD	*From Monday 5th to Sunday 25th January 2026*	*Prayer Centers all over the world*

SCHOOL OF PRAYER 2026			
50 NIGHTS OF POWER 2026	Join us for the 2nd edition of the **SCHOOL OF PRAYER**	Date	*Prepare to be part of this life-changing encounter*
		From Saturday 1st February to Saturday 22nd March 2026	

SPECIAL PROGRAM: I PRAY FOR YOU
Join Pastor Godson for a half hour morning devotion **every MONDAY, WEDNESDAY, and FRIDAY** from **6am** live on Facebook, YouTube **@PastorGodsonNemboTangumonkem**

HOUR OF RESTORATION
Join Pastor Godson & Anna TANGUMONKEM for HOUR OF RESTORATION **every TUESDAY** morning from **6 – 7:30am** in the banquet hall: Salle des fêtes « Fontaine de grâce » at Jouvence, Mendong street – Yaounde, Cameroon.. *A time of prophetic intercession for individuals, families and the nations.*

ANNOUNCEMENTS

- Festival of Fire series No. 1-5 and Power Must Change Hands Vol. 1-10 now available at XAF 3,000. Send your orders from today.
- Annual subscription to the Daily Prayer Guide from XAF 10,000 for electronic copies.
- All our books are available at our CRN Head office: 1st Floor Storey Building at Entrée Lycée de Tsinga village on the edge of the main road. **Contact:** 681.72.24.04, 695.72.23.40
- Carmel Credit Union, Yaoundé branch located at Carrefour Biyem-Assi, on the ground floor of the storey building, opposite Campus Crusade for Christ. **Contact:** +237 652.83.55.04
- Prayer Storm Bookshop at Cow Street Nkwen – Bamenda sells our books, Bibles and excellent Christian literature. **Contact:** 675.14.04.50, 674.59.35.98, 679.46.57.17.

"RESTORATION CAMP" Project

- The project for the establishment of the base for CRN in Yaounde, Cameroon began in January 2020.
- The LAYING OF THE FOUNDATION STONE FOR THE RESTORATION PRAYER HOUSE at Tsinga Village, Yaounde, took place in December 2023.
- For information on how to be part of the project, call or send SMS to **(237) 674.49.58.95, 678.16.46.88, 673.50.42.33, 699.90.26.18.**

Feedback Questionnaire:
We will love to hear your suggestions on how we can improve on this book: Send your comments to **(237) 681722404**, use the link https://prayer-stormdevotional.paperform.com/ or scan the QR CODE shown here to fill the online form.

HOW TO BECOME A CHILD OF GOD

Going to church and praying is not enough. *"Except a man is BORN AGAIN, he CANNOT SEE the kingdom of God." (John 3:3).*
The following steps will help you know how you can be born again.

Step 1: God Loves You and Offers a Wonderful Plan for Your Life
"For God so loved the world that He gave His only begotten Son, that whoever believes in Him should not perish but have everlasting life" (John 3:16). Jesus said, *"I came that they might have life and have it to the full." (John 10:10).*
No matter who you are and what you have done, God still loves you and wants to save you (Rom.5:8).

Step 2: Your Sins Have Separated You from God; That Is Why You Are Not Experiencing His Wonderful Plan for Your Life
"For all have sinned and fall short of the glory of God" (Rom.3:23) "The wages of sin is death (spiritual separation from God) Rom.6:23.
All your religious activities and efforts cannot save you. God has provided a solution for you.

Step 3: Jesus Christ Is the Only Way Back to God
Jesus said, *"I am the way, the truth and the life, No one comes to the father except through me" (John 14:6).* Jesus is the only sacrifice God can accept for your sins. Through Him you can connect to God's plan for your life.

Step 4: You Must Personally Receive Jesus Christ as Your Saviour and Lord. Then You Can Know and Experience God's Plan for Your Life

Receive Him by personal invitation and by faith. *"Behold, I stand at the door and knock. If anyone hears My voice and opens the door (your heart), I will come in to him and dine with him, and he with Me." (Rev.3:20).*

If you are ready now to give your life to Jesus Christ, pray this prayer with all your heart.

"Dear Lord Jesus Christ, I need you. I open the door of my life and receive you as my Saviour and Lord. Forgive all my sins and wash me with your blood. Make me the kind of person you want me to be. Thank you for saving me."

Congrats! You are now a child of God.

Call us now let us pray for you: (237) 652.38.26.93 or 696.56.58.64

(Pastor Godson T. Nembo & Prayer Storm Team)

NOW THAT YOU ARE BORN AGAIN

Making the decision to become a born-again Christian, is the best decision you've ever made in your entire life and I congratulate you for that. The following points will help you enjoy your newfound life in Christ Jesus.

1. **Live with the Consciousness that You are Saved:** It is fundamental that you are certain of your new faith. This is referred to as the Assurance of Salvation. Believe that your sins have been forgiven and forgotten by God because of the price Jesus paid by His sacrificial death on the cross and that you are no longer under any condemnation (Acts 16:31, Rom.8:1-2, 2Cor.5:17, Jn.1:12).

2. **Join a Fellowship:** By new birth, you have entered the family of God. Locate a church that teaches and practises the scriptures truthfully, where the worship enables you to encounter God, and where the people are friendly and spiritual growth is encouraged (Heb.10:25, Gal.6:10).

3. **Get a Bible and Study It Daily:** You can begin from John, then Acts, Romans, etc. Just as a baby needs physical nourishment in order to grow, the Word of God is also the spiritual food by which we grow into Christlikeness (1Pet.2:2, Jn.5:24). Consult other mature Christians for any explanations.

4. **Commune Daily with God:** Through prayer, we talk with God, express our burdens to Him, as well as offer worship, praise and appreciation. We also have the privilege to get God speak to us, showering upon us His

love, peace, blessings and divine direction (Rom.10:9, 1Thess.5:17, 1Pet.5:8).

5. **Destroy Satan's Property in Your Keeping:** Desist from anything that does not glorify God. Do away with anything evil related to your sinful past, such as pornographic materials, stolen money and possessions, talismans, charms, juju, etc. (2Cor.6:17, Tit.2:11).

6. **Separate from Evil Friends and Get New Godly Friends:** Now that you are born again, you must discontinue the former way of life and walk in the truth (Ps.1:1-3, 2Cor.4:2; 5:17, Eph.4:22, 1Jn.1:6).

7. **Get Baptized:** Water baptism by immersion publicly authenticates our salvation and affirms our membership in the body of Christ (Rom.6:4, Col.2:12, Matt.28:19, Acts 2:38, 8:36).

8. **Seek the Baptism of the Holy Spirit:** The Holy Spirit assures us that we are saved and empowers us to live a holy life and do exploits for God through special gifts (Rom.8:14, Acts 2:1-4; 10:38, Eph.5:18).

9. **Tell Others about Jesus:** Our character should testify about our inner transformation. Also, our eagerness to tell others about God's love and lead them to Christ is also evidential about our salvation (Jn.4:28-29, Acts 4:10; 22:14, 2Tim.2:2).

10. **Worship God with Your Wealth through Offerings and Tithes:** Our cheerful giving is essential in advancing God's Kingdom – freewill offerings and tithe (one-tenth

of our increase) (Deut.16:16-17, Prov.3:9-10, 2Cor:9:7).

11. **Make the Life of Christ Your Standard:** Fix your eyes on Jesus, the Author and Finisher of our faith Make Him your Role Model (Heb.12:2, Phil.2:5-11, Eph.4:24).

12. **Don't Abandon; Rise and Continue, if you Fall:** The Christian race may seem tough and challenging, with persecutions, distractions, oppositions, and even discouragements. But rest assured, you will make it by faith (Prov.24:16, Isa.41:10, Phil.1:6).

I pray that you will stand firm, and finish well like other heroes of faith, in Jesus' name! Amen.

Call us for counselling and prayer: (237) 652.38.26.93 or 696.56.58.64.

(Pastor Godson T. Nembo & Prayer Storm Team)

HOW TO USE THIS DAILY PRAYER GUIDE

I have discovered that some people do not know how to use this book well. As a result, they are not benefiting much from it. I will like to explain to you, how you can either use it during your personal prayer time or how to use it to lead a group prayer session.

Your Personal Prayer Time:
1. ***Read the topic of the day:*** It is the summary of the message of the day.
2. ***Read the Bible passages of the day aloud:*** You retain more, when you read aloud to yourself. In the early days, scriptures were read aloud.
3. ***Read the meditation slowly:*** Do it with a strong desire to understand.
4. ***Pray the prayer points:*** Read each prayer point and take time to pray well before you read the next one.
5. ***Pray for others:*** Use the prayer point to pray for other people as inspired by the Holy Spirit.
6. ***Add other prayer topics:*** For instance; dedicate your day, your family, your job, your Church, etc. to God.
7. Pray for your specific needs and those of others.
8. ***Action/Declaration:*** Take practical steps and do the prophetic declarations.
9. ***Prophetic Prayers of the Week:*** These prayers will be brought up every Monday. We encourage you to pray them every day during the week that follows.

Leading a Group to Pray:
1. Read the topic of the day aloud.
2. Assign one or more persons to read the Bible passage of

the day aloud.
3. Read the meditation of the day aloud. After reading, you can make some comments, if necessary.
4. Allow other members of the group to make contributions or ask questions, if they have them.
5. Read one prayer point at a time. Then allow the people to pray for some time before you read the next one.
6. After they have prayed in chorus, you can ask one person to raise his/her voice and pray.
7. When you finish reading the prayer points, first ask the group members to give their own personal prayer plan.
8. At the end, let one person pray and conclude the session.

Bible Reading Plan:

We have included two Bible reading plans: **"Bible in 1 year"** and **"Bible in 2 years."** You can read through your Bible in one year by following the first plan in two years by following the second plan. Set aside time every day to read your Bible.

Thursday 1 January   **THE FOUNDATION FOR ENLARGEMENT**

Read: Isaiah 54:1-5

Bible in 1 year: Prov. 1-3
Bible in 2 years: Gen. 1-2

"Enlarge the place of your tent, and let them stretch out the curtains of your dwellings; do not spare; lengthen your cords, and strengthen your stakes" (Isaiah 54:2).

Happy New Year! The prophetic mandate for 2026 is "ENLARGED BY GOD." The scripture calls us to intentionally prepare for this increase with this instruction: *"Enlarge the place of your tent."* This is a call to action, but true enlargement begins not with external hustle, but with internal alignment – a deepening of intimacy with God through prayer and fasting, rooted in His living Word.

In today's text, the prophet Isaiah speaks to those who were once "barren" (vs. 1). He promises a season of breakthrough and multiplication. However, multiplication demands preparation. Without action, expectation ends in frustration. As God commands, when we stretch out the curtains and lengthen the cords of our spiritual "tent," we are making room for His blessings before they arrive. Consecration, prayer, and fasting are the primary tools you need to position yourself for what God wants to do.

Every tree goes through three stages: the seed stage, the tree stage, and the fruit stage. God's ultimate vision for you is that you attain the fruit stage, where the gifts, talents, and blessings He has deposited in you will produce impactful results. Praying and fasting to see this happen indicates that you cannot make it without God.

Enlargement is the promise, but Intimacy is the prerequisite. Through focused intimacy, you will allow the Holy Spirit to incubate you, just as He did to Mary (Luke 1). This divine covering will activate clarity, revealing hidden strategies for a victorious and profitable life in 2026.

When you start your year in prayer and fasting, you are building a spiritual foundation strong enough to handle the expansion God is sending your way, ensuring your growth is sustainable, God-ordained, and fruitful. Make your primary goal this January to secure the divine blueprint for your year.

Action: *Establish a prayer and fasting program to pray and take over the year 2026, or join the program in your church.*

Let us pray

1. *Father, thank You for the prophetic word of enlargement over my life in 2026, in Jesus' name.*
2. *Holy Spirit, stir up an intense hunger for intimacy with You through prayer and the Word, in Jesus' name.*
3. *I receive the grace to be disciplined in prayer and fasting this season for divine direction, in Jesus' name.*
4. *Lord, reveal to me the specific areas of my life (my "tent") that I must stretch out and prepare for Your incoming blessing, in Jesus' name.*
5. *I surrender my will and my plans to You; grant me clarity and direction to walk only in Your divine blueprint for my enlargement this year, in Jesus' name.*

SPECIAL PRAYER STORM PROGRAM
21 DAYS FASTING AND PRAYER
to take over the year.
Theme: **ENLARGED BY GOD.**
Date: Monday 5 – Sunday 25 January 2025.
(Prepare yourself to join us).

Friday 2 January **ENLARGED IN THE SECRET PLACE**

Read: Luke 5:12-16

> **Bible in 1 year:** Prov. 4-7
> **Bible in 2 years:** Gen. 3-4

"But Jesus often withdrew to lonely places and prayed" (Luke 5:16 NIV).

Intimacy with God in the secret place is key to divine enlargement. You must undergo spiritual incubation for impartation to manifest your destiny. Naturally, no woman can become pregnant and give birth to children without intimacy with her husband.

Crowds pressed around Jesus daily, hungry for miracles, yet He continually withdrew to pray. He understood that fruitfulness in His ministry flowed from intimacy with His Father, not activity. He said, *"Very truly I tell you, the Son can do nothing by himself; he can do only what he sees his Father doing, because whatever the Father does the Son also does" (John 5:19)*. Where did He see the things His Father was doing? When He went to interact with Him in prayer. Today, many believers want expansion – bigger ministries, influence, breakthroughs, but neglect the quiet places with God where enlargement truly begins.

Intimacy is not isolation; it is connection. When Jesus retreated to the Father, He wasn't escaping duty; He was refilling His soul and charging up for impact. The more He drew near, the more power flowed out of Him. His miracles were born in those unseen conversations with His Father.

Years ago, my ministry was transformed when I began to withdraw every Monday and spend the whole day with God. I always returned home recharged and empowered to serve God better. I developed the ability to hear God more clearly during those quiet moments in the prayer house.

The Greek word for "withdrew" in Luke 5:16 is *'Hupochoreo,'* meaning "To move back under divine direction." It's not retreating in fear, but repositioning for strength. Every time you step back into God's presence, He pushes you forward with renewed power. Hallelujah!

Your enlargement will come this year through your secret place. The more time you spend with Jesus, the more space He creates in you to carry His glory.

Action: *Spend at least thirty quiet minutes alone with God daily before you talk to anyone else!*

Let us pray
1. *Father, thank You for inviting me into Your presence and enlarging my heart with Your love, in Jesus' name.*
2. *Father, teach me to value time alone with You more than public approval, in Jesus' name.*
3. *I break every distraction that keeps me from deep fellowship with God, in Jesus' name.*
4. *Father, enlarge my capacity to hear, obey, and reflect Christ daily, in Jesus' name.*
5. *I decree that this year, my influence, wisdom, and fruitfulness shall expand through intimacy with God, in Jesus' name.*

Saturday 3 January **LENGTHEN THE CORD OF PRAYER**

Read: Jeremiah 29:11-13

> **Bible in 1 year:** Prov. 8-11
> **Bible in 2 years:** Gen. 5-6

"You will seek Me and find Me, when you search for Me with all your heart." (Jeremiah 29:13).

The other day, we embraced the prophetic mandate to "Enlarge the place of our tents," an act that requires us to stretch the curtains and strengthen the stakes. Spiritually, the cord that connects us to the Father and allows for this magnificent expansion is our prayer life. The Lord calls us to "lengthen your cords," and the extent of our divine enlargement this year is directly proportional to the length and intensity of this spiritual connection.

Jeremiah 29:11 promises a future filled with hope and a plan for our increase, but verse 13 reveals the pathway to accessing that plan: TOTAL DEDICATION. *"You will seek Me and find Me, when you search for Me WITH ALL YOUR HEART."* This divine invitation highlights the reciprocal nature of intimacy: when we pursue God wholly, He ensures we find the direction we need.

Starting the year with prayer and fasting is the spiritual equivalent of committing to an "all your heart" pursuit. Fasting elevates our sincerity, demonstrating to God that we value His presence and direction above our natural comfort and needs. It is in this place of deep consecration that the Holy Spirit begins to communicate the precise steps for our enlargement. We are not meant to enlarge our tent blindly; we must move according to God's strategic, Divine Direction.

The search for God with "all your heart" is the gateway to receiving the intelligence and wisdom that human effort cannot provide. Resolve today to lengthen the cord of prayer; dedicate yourself to seeking Him with a focused heart, and watch as your obedience unlocks the promise of enlargement in 2026.

Action: *Set a specific time today to pray longer and specifically ask God for a strategic plan for this year!*

Let us pray
1. *Father, I thank You for the great plans and divine enlargement You have for me, in Jesus' name.*
2. *Holy Spirit, grant me the strength and discipline to lengthen the cord of my prayer life this month, in Jesus' name.*
3. *I commit to seeking You with all my heart; grant me the grace to find the exact direction I need for my enlargement, in Jesus' name.*
4. *I silence every internal and external distraction that competes with my time of intimacy with You, in Jesus' name.*
5. *Lord, may my fasting this month amplify my spiritual hearing so I receive the strategic blueprints for 2026, in Jesus' name.*
6. *I receive the anointing for persistent, focused prayer that secures and sustains my promised enlargement, in Jesus' name.*

Sunday 4 January **THE CALL TO ABIDE**

Read: John 15:1-8

> **Bible in 1 year:** Prov. 12-14
> **Bible in 2 years:** Gen. 7-8

"Abide in Me, and I in you. As the branch cannot bear fruit of itself unless it abides in the vine, neither can you, unless you abide in Me" (John 15:4).

Fruitfulness in the Kingdom is a by-product of our fellowship with God through Jesus Christ. In our text, Jesus compares our relationship with Him to a vine and its branches. Hence, fruitfulness is never a product of effort; it is the outcome of intimacy.

Unfortunately, today, many believers are active yet spiritually dry because they try to bear fruit without abiding. Jesus invites you to a deeper place – not of more work, but of more connection.

"Abide" is Greek *'Meno'*, which means "To stay, remain, or dwell continuously." It implies consistency rather than visits. Dear friend, God enlarges those who remain rooted in His presence, not those who stop by only occasionally. To abide is to remain, to make your home in Christ. It means allowing His words to shape your thoughts, His Spirit to fill your heart, and His love to motivate every action you make.

When you dwell in Him, your capacity enlarges – your patience deepens, your joy stabilizes, and your spiritual influence increases. Paul lived this truth. He declared, *"It is no longer I who live, but Christ lives in me" (Galatians 2:20).* His ministry's power flowed from intimacy, not status – his title.

Beloved in the Lord, you must discover this spiritual truth: your fruitfulness and enlargement depend on your consistency in Christ. You stop being that Christian who is spiritual in Church but disconnects from the Holy Spirit once out of Church. You must stay in God's presence everywhere you go. Become conscious that you are God's mobile temple (1 Corinthians 3:16). You don't go to meet with God in Church, you go with God to Church to fellowship with your brethren.

Stop searching for God; He is with you. Start abiding in Him deeper as you focus on Jesus Christ.

Action: *Throughout today, use every free time you have to read, meditate, pray, or listen to worship music!*

Let us pray

1. *Father, thank You for calling me to abide in You and for making Your presence my dwelling, in Jesus' name.*
2. *Lord, help me remain rooted in Christ, even when I feel dry or tired, in Jesus' name.*
3. *Father, let Your Word take deeper roots in my heart and bear lasting fruit, in Jesus' name.*
4. *O Lord, enlarge my inner strength to remain steadfast and fruitful through intimacy, in Jesus' name.*
5. *I decree that my life shall overflow with divine fruit because I abide continually in Christ, in Jesus' name.*

PRAYER TOPICS for the 21-DAY FAST to take over 2026 – 05 to 25 Jan. 2026

Here are the prayer topics we will use for the 21-day fast. Manage them as you are inspired.

A. Thanksgiving:

1. *"Give thanks to the Lord, for he is good" (Psalm 107:1)* - Lord, I thank You for Your mighty hand of enlargement at work in my life this year, in Jesus' name.

2. *"His mercies are new every morning" (Lamentations 3:23* - Father, thank You for Your daily mercies and unending love, in Jesus' name.

3. *"The Lord will fight for you" (Exodus 14:14)* - Father, thank You for fighting battles and for not allowing my enemies to wipe me out, in Jesus' name.

4. *"He will command his angels concerning you" (Psalm 91:11)* - Father, thank You for divine protection over my family in Jesus' name.

5. *"He who opens and no one shuts" (Revelation 3:7)*- Father, thank You for the doors You are opening for me this year, in Jesus' name.

6. *"My God will supply all your needs" (Philippians 4:19)* - Father, thank You because You will supply all my needs this year, in Jesus' name.

7. *"I shall not die, but live" (Ps. 118:17)* – Faithful Father, thank You because You will preserve us this year, in Jesus' name.

B. Repentance:

8. *"Create in me a clean heart, O God" (Psalm 51:10)* - Lord, cleanse my heart from every hidden sin, in Jesus' name.

9. *"Lord, I believe; help my unbelief" (Mark 9:24)* - Father, forgive my unbelief and strengthen my faith in Jesus' name.
10. *"If we confess…He is faithful to forgive" (1 John 1:9)* - Merciful Father, wash me from every iniquity that can hinder my enlargement this year, in Jesus' name.
11. *"Sin shall not have dominion over you" (Romans 6:14)* - Father, deliver me from every sinful habit in Jesus' name.
12. *"Let the meditation of my heart be acceptable" (Psalm 19:14)* - Lord, purge my thoughts and my motives in Jesus' name.
13. *"The spirit is willing, but the flesh is weak" (Matthew 26:41)* - Father, remove every spiritual weakness in me, in Jesus' name.

C. Consecration:

14. *"Be holy, for I am holy" (Peter 1:16)* - Lord, set my heart apart for Your glory, in Jesus' name.
15. *"A vessel for honor, sanctified" (2 Timothy 2:21)* - Father, make me a vessel of honor, in Jesus' name.
16. *"You have loved righteousness and hated wickedness" (Hebrews 1:9)* - Lord, help me to love righteousness and hate sin, in Jesus' name.
17. *"Your will be done" (Matthew 6:10)* - Father, align my desires with Your will throughout this year, in Jesus' name.
18. *"Blessed are the pure in heart" (Matthew 5:8)* - Lord, strengthen me to walk in purity and truth this year, in Jesus' name.
19. *"Without holiness no one will see the Lord" (Hebrews 12:14)* - Father, let my life reflect Your holiness, in Jesus' name.
20. *"Deny ungodliness and worldly lusts" (Titus 2:12)* - Lord, empower me to say no to ungodliness, in Jesus' name.

21. *"The work of their hands you bless" (Psalm 90:17)* - Father, consecrate my hands for good works, in Jesus' name.
22. *"Let the word of Christ dwell in you richly" (Colossians 3:16)* - Lord, saturate my thoughts with Your Word, in Jesus' name.

D. Breakthrough:

23. 23*"You shall break out on the right and on the left" (Isaiah 54:3)* - Lord, break every limitation placed on my destiny, in Jesus' name.
24. *"Knock, and it will be opened" (Matthew 7:7)* - Father, let every closed door open for me this year in Jesus' name.
25. *"Is my word not like a hammer?" (Jeremiah 23:29)* - Lord, let every barrier to my enlargement and my family members be shattered, in Jesus' name.
26. *"The hand of the Lord came upon Elijah…and he ran" (1 Kings 18:46)* - Lord, release grace for acceleration upon my life, in Jesus' name.
27. *"Time and chance happen to them all" (Ecclesiastes 9:11)* - Father, let unusual opportunities locate me this year, in Jesus' name.
28. *"The Lord makes poor and makes rich" (1 Samuel 2:7)* - Lord, enlarge my financial territory this year, in Jesus' name.
29. *"Thanks be to God who gives us victory" (1 Corinthians 15:57)* - Father, give me victory over every stubborn problem, in Jesus' name.
30. *"Behold, I will do a new thing" (Isaiah 43:19)* - Father, command a new chapter to open for family and me from this year, in Jesus' name.

E. Security:
31. *"'I will be a wall of fire around her,' declares the Lord" (Zechariah 2:5)* - Lord, build a wall of fire around my family and me, in Jesus' name.
32. *"He will cover you with his feathers" (Psalm 91:4)* - Father, hide us under Your wings in this year, in Jesus' name.
33. *"He frustrates the plans of the wicked" (Psalm 146:9)* - Father, frustrate every evil plan intended to stop my progress in Jesus' name.
34. *"The Lord is faithful…He will protect you from the evil one" (2 Thessalonians 3:3)* - Father, shield us from every spiritual attack assigned against our destinies, in Jesus' name.
35. *"He will command his angels concerning you" (Psalm 91:11)* - Father, let Your angels guard my going out and coming in today, in Jesus' name.
36. *"When I see the blood, I will pass over you" (Exodus 12:13)* - Father, surround my dwelling with the blood of Jesus daily, in Jesus' name.
37. *"He delivers you from the snare of the fowler" (Psalm 91:3)* - Father, deliver me from every snare of the enemy, in Jesus' name.
38. *"They shall surely gather…but not by Me" (Isaiah 54:15)* - Lord, scatter every evil gathering against my enlargement, in Jesus' name.
39. *"You will not fear the terror of night" (Psalm 91:5)* - Father, preserve my life from sudden destruction, in Jesus' name.

F. Vision:
40. *"Open my eyes that I may see" (Psalm 119:18)* - Lord, open my eyes to see the great future You have prepared for me, in Jesus' name.

41. *"Call… I will show you great and mighty things"* (Jeremiah 33:3) - Father, give me divine insight for my next level this year, in Jesus' name.
42. *"Write the vision and make it plain"* (Habakkuk 2:2) - Lord, enlarge my capacity to dream big, in Jesus' name.
43. *"Where there is no vision, the people perish"* (Proverbs 29:18) - Father, let every blurred spiritual vision be restored, in Jesus' name.
44. *"The veil is taken away in Christ"* (2 Corinthians 3:14) - Father, remove every veil covering my spiritual understanding, in Jesus' name.
45. *"Your eyes shall see the King in His beauty"* (Isaiah 33:17) - Father, align my vision with Heaven's agenda this year, in Jesus' name.
46. *"In all your ways acknowledge Him"* (Proverbs 3:6) - Father, show me where You want to enlarge me this year, in Jesus' name.
47. *"Lift up your eyes and look"* (John 4:35) - Lord, reveal the opportunities around me that I have not seen, in Jesus' name.
48. *"Be strong and courageous"* (Joshua 1:9) - Father, grant me boldness to pursue divine visions in Jesus' name.

G. Divine Direction:

49. *"For as many as are led by the Spirit…"* (Romans 8:14) - Lord, lead me by Your Spirit into my place of enlargement, in Jesus' name.
50. *"The steps of a good man are ordered by the Lord"* (Psalm 37:23) - Father, guide my decisions and steps this year, in Jesus' name.

51. *"Bad company ruins good morals" (1 Corinthians 15:33)* - Lord, keep me from wrong paths and wrong associations, in Jesus' name.
52. *"My sheep hear my voice" (John 10:27)* - Father, silence every voice contradicting Your direction in my life, in Jesus' name.
53. *"A great and effectual door has opened" (1 Corinthians 16:9)* - Lord, show me the right door to enter for my enlargement this year, in Jesus' name.
54. *"There is a way that seems right…" (Proverbs 14:12)* - Father, direct me away from paths that lead to loss, in Jesus' name.
55. *"Your word is a lamp to my feet" (Psalm 119:105)* - Lord, let Your word be a light on my path, in Jesus' name.
56. *"In all your ways submit to him" (Proverbs 3:6)* - Father, help me to choose according to Your will, not my emotions, in Jesus' name.
57. *"Two are better than one" (Ecclesiastes 4:9)* - Lord, connect me to destiny helpers who will propel my enlargement in Jesus' name.
58. *"You shall go out with joy and be led forth with peace" (Isaiah 55:12)* - Father, lead me by peace in all my decisions, in Jesus' name.

H. Love & Intimacy With God
59. *"You shall love the Lord your God" (Matthew 22:37)* - Lord, enlarge my love for You above everything else, in Jesus' name.
60. *Draw near to God, and He will draw near to you" (James 4:8)* - Father, draw me deeper into Your presence daily, in Jesus' name.

61. *"The fervent prayer a righteous person avails much" (James 5:16)* - Lord, restore the fire of prayer and worship in my heart, in Jesus' name.
62. *"If you love me, keep my commands" (John 14:15)* - Father, give me grace to obey You joyfully always, in Jesus' name.
63. *"Blessed are those who hunger…for they shall be filled" (Matthew 5:6)* - Lord, deepen my hunger for righteousness, in Jesus' name.
64. *"One thing I ask…that I may dwell in Your house" (Psalm 27:4)* - Father, make intimacy with You my highest priority, in Jesus' name.
65. *"He speaks in a still small voice" (1 Kings 19:12)* - Father, teach me to hear and recognize Your voice clearly in Jesus' name.

I. Healing & Health
66. *"I will restore health to you" (Jeremiah 30:17)* – Father, cause me to enjoy unlimited divine healing and health this year, in Jesus' name.
67. *"By His stripes you are healed." — Isaiah 53:5* - Father, let every sickness in my body dry up now, in Jesus' name.
68. *"The joy of the Lord is your strength" (Nehemiah 8:10)* - Lord, strengthen me spiritually, physically, and mentally, in Jesus' name.
69. *"No plague shall come near your dwelling" (Psalm 91:10)* - Father, protect us from diseases and infirmities, in Jesus' name.
70. *"He renews your youth like the eagle's" (Psalm 103:5)* - Lord, renew my youth like the eagle's, in Jesus' name.

J. Angelic Ministry:

71. *"Are they not ministering spirits?" (Hebrews 1:14)* - Lord, release Your angels to guide and guard my path, in Jesus' name.
72. *"An angel touched him…" (1 Kings 19:5)* - Father, let angelic assistance speed up my breakthroughs this year, in Jesus' name.
73. *"The angel of the Lord encamps around them" (Psalm 34:7)* - Lord, let warring angels fight unseen battles for me, in Jesus' name.

K. Marriage for Singles:

74. *"No good thing will He withhold…" (Psalm 84:11)* - Lord, settle me maritally this year, in Jesus' name.
75. *"He sets the solitary in families." (Psalm 68:6)* - Father, connect me divinely to my God-ordained spouse, in Jesus' name.
76. *"The blessing of the Lord makes rich…" (Proverbs 10:22)* - Father, remove every marital delay around my life, in Jesus' name.

L. Married Couples:

77. *"Two are better than one…" (Ecclesiastes 4:9)* - Father, give us grace to support each other faithfully, in Jesus' name.
78. *"Love never fails." (1 Corinthians 13:8)* - Lord, restore love, joy, and peace in every home, in Jesus' name.
79. *"A threefold cord is not quickly broken." (Ecclesiastes 4:12)* - Jesus, be the center of our marriage, in Jesus' name.
80. *"Let all bitterness… be put away." (Ephesians 4:31)* - Father, heal every wound and dissolve every conflict in my home, in Jesus' name.
81. *"The Lord will perfect that which concerns me." (Psalm 138:8)* - Lord, perfect our marriage in every area, in Jesus' name.

M. Household:
82. *"As for me and my house…"* *(Joshua 24:15)* - Father, establish Your lordship in our family, in Jesus' name.
83. *"Great shall be the peace of your children."* *(Isaiah 54:13)* - Lord, release divine peace into every household, in Jesus' name.
84. *"I and the children… are for signs."* *(Isaiah 8:18)* - Father, make every family member a sign and wonder, in Jesus' name.
85. *"The Lord surrounds His people."* *(Psalm 125:2)* - Lord, surround our families with protection, in Jesus' name.
86. *"The righteous will flourish."* *(Psalm 92:12)* - Father, let our families flourish spiritually and materially, in Jesus' name.

N. Missionaries
87. *"Go…and I am with you."* *(Matthew 28:19-20)* - Lord, be with our missionaries and strengthen them daily, in Jesus' name.
88. *"The Lord is my light…"* *(Psalm 27:1)* - Father, protect our missionaries from danger and darkness, in Jesus' name.
89. *"My God shall supply all your need."* *(Philippians 4:19)* - Lord, provide every financial and material need of our missionaries, in Jesus' name.
90. *"Open to us a door…"* *(Colossians 4:3)* - Father, grant open doors for souls and breakthroughs in missions this year, in Jesus' name.
91. *"Those who sow in tears…"* *(Psalm 126:5)* - Lord, let their labor produce great harvests in 2026, in Jesus' name.

O. Spiritual Revival in the Nation
92. *"Will You not revive us again?"* *(Psalm 85:6)* - Father, pour out Your fire of revival on our nation, in Jesus' name.

93. *"Arise, shine…" (Isaiah 60:1)* - Lord, let Your light dispel every spiritual darkness over this nation, in Jesus' name.
94. *"I will pour out My Spirit…" (Joel 2:28)* - Father, release a fresh outpouring of Your Spirit across churches, in Jesus' name.
95. *"Righteousness exalts a nation." (Proverbs 14:34)* - Lord, restore righteousness and holiness in the land, in Jesus' name.
96. *"Let God arise…" (Psalm 68:1)* - Father, let every anti-revival force scatter, in Jesus' name.

P. Victory Over Terrorism:
97. *"He is my fortress." (Psalm 91:2)* - Lord, shield our nation from every terrorist attack, in Jesus' name.
98. *"No weapon… shall prosper." (Isaiah 54:17)* - Father, frustrate every plan of terrorists, in Jesus' name.
99. *"The Lord is a man of war." (Exodus 15:3)* - Lord, arise and fight against violent men, in Jesus' name.
100. *"He makes wars cease." (Psalm 46:9)* - Father, silence every operation of wickedness, in Jesus' name.
101. *"The wicked will perish." (Psalm 37:20)* – Father, arise, let every terror network collapse, in Jesus' name.

Q. Peace in the Nations:
102. *"My peace I give you." (John 14:27)* - Lord, release supernatural peace upon every troubled nation, in Jesus' name.
103. *"Blessed are the peacemakers."* (Matthew 5:9) - Father, raise peacemakers and wise leaders globally, in Jesus' name.
104. *"Pray for the peace of Jerusalem." (Psalm 122:6)* - Lord, establish lasting peace in every region of conflict, in Jesus' name.

105. *"Let the God of peace crush Satan."* *(Romans 16:20)* - Father, crush the root of unrest and violence, in Jesus' name.
106. *"He makes peace in your borders."* *(Psalm 147:14)* - Lord, secure the borders of nations with Your peace, in Jesus' name.

Monday 5 January **ENLARGED THROUGH OBEDIENCE**

Read: Genesis 12:1-4

Bible in 1 year: Prov. 15-18
Bible in 2 years: Gen. 9-10

"He who has My commandments and keeps them, it is he who loves Me. And he who loves Me will be loved by My Father, and I will love him and manifest Myself to him" (John 14:21).

Many people desire a deeper experience of God and His blessings, but intimacy with Him is not built only through prayer and worship; it is proven through obedience. Jesus said that love for Him is demonstrated by doing what He commands (John 14:15). How can you claim to love Him but refuse to obey Him?

Obedience opens the door to revelation. Every time you obey, you make room for God to manifest Himself in your life. And wherever God abides, there is freedom, peace, and increase (2 Corinthians 3:17).

A powerful example of divine enlargement through obedience is Abraham. When God called him to leave his country, family, and security to go to an unknown land, he obeyed without hesitation. His act of obedience by faith opened the door to generational blessings – God blessed him, made his name great, and made his family a great nation. His obedience not only enlarged his life but also became the foundation for God's redemptive plan through Jesus Christ (Galatians 3:8-9). Abraham's story reminds us that enlargement is always tied to obedience. When we trust and follow God's instructions, even when they seem unclear, He positions us for increase beyond our imagination. Do you want to expand this year? Obey God's instructions promptly and fully!

When Jesus obeyed the Father, even unto death, He didn't lose; He was enlarged. The cross looked like a loss, but it led to resurrection power and worldwide redemption. Likewise, your obedience may cost you comfort, pride, or convenience, but it enlarges your spiritual authority. Paul understood this when he said, *"Though He was a Son, yet He learned obedience by the things which He suffered" (Hebrews 5:8)*. That same process will deepen your intimacy with God; it will turn head knowledge into heart experience.

One day, somebody mistakenly sent a large sum of money into the account of a young Christian entrepreneur. Though tempted to keep it, she obeyed God and returned the money. A few weeks later, she received an unexpected business contract worth ten times more.

This year, obedience will enlarge your capacity to experience God more. Your enlargement begins the moment you say "Yes" to God's command.

Action: *Choose one area where God has been prompting you to obey, and act on it today without delay.*

Let us pray
1. *Father, thank You because You manifest Your love and You reveal Yourself to those who obey, in Jesus' name.*
2. *Father, give me a willing heart to obey You promptly and fully, in Jesus' name.*

3. O Father, deliver me from fear and pride that resist Your instructions, in Jesus' name.
4. Father, let every act of obedience unlock deeper intimacy and favor in my life and family, in Jesus's name.
5. Father, enlarge my spirit to value Your Word above personal comfort, in Jesus' name.
6. I decree that my obedience will produce divine enlargement and visible manifestations of God's presence in my life this year, in Jesus' name.

Prophetic Prayers of the Week

1. **"Enlarge the place of your tent." (Isaiah 54:2)** *My capacity is enlarged on every side, in Jesus' name.*
2. **"I will increase you more and more." (Psalm 115:14)** *I will enjoy divine increase everywhere I go this year, in Jesus' name.*
3. **"Your latter end will greatly increase." (Job 8:7)** *Small things in my life will greatly increase this year, in Jesus' name.*

Tuesday 6 January **LET THE HOLY SPIRIT INCUBATE YOU**

Read: Luke 1:26-38

Bible in 1 year: Prov. 19-21
Bible in 2 years: Gen. 11-12

"The Holy Spirit will come upon you, and the power of the Most High will overshadow you. So the baby to be born will be holy, and he will be called the Son of God" (Luke 1:35 NLT).

There is no divine manifestation without divine impartation. Before something extraordinary is born through you, something holy must be formed inside you. The Bible says, *"The Holy Spirit will come upon you, and the power of the Most-High will overshadow you."*

The Greek word for "Overshadow" is *'Episkiazo'*, meaning "To envelop in a haze of brilliance" or "To cover with influence." It depicts a hen covering her eggs until life forms within them. That's what the Holy Spirit did to Mary before she became pregnant and gave birth to Jesus. He covered her, filled her, and infused her with divine life. When the Spirit overshadows you, your natural limitations and impossibilities are covered by supernatural possibilities.

Mary's divine encounter teaches us that divine incubation produces divine, indisputable results. Prophecies are activated. Isaiah 9:6 was a prophecy concerning a virgin, which was fulfilled in her life because she yielded to the Holy Spirit: *"For unto us a Child is born, unto us a Son is given; and the government will be upon His shoulder."* Through her obedience, the world received the Savior. There are prophecies waiting to be fulfilled in this generation. May your alignment with the Holy Spirit like Mary, make you a channel of manifestation, in Jesus' name.

It was during the thirty-day annual fast in 2010 that the Holy Spirit overshadowed me and I heard His voice, "My people want to pray, but they don't know how to do it. Write a prayer guide to help them." This is how the Prayer Storm Daily Prayer Guide was born. Today, it has transformed the lives of multitudes globally. When the Holy Spirit incubates you, you begin to give birth to God's ideas, not your own.

Mary was quietly serving God when grace located her. She simply believed and surrendered: *"Let it be to me according to your word" (v. 38)*. If you will remain humble, pure, and yielded, the Spirit will overshadow you too, and what is conceived in you will bless generations.

Action: *Focus on praying in tongues today — do it as long as possible!*

Let us pray
1. *Father, thank You for the gift and presence of Your Holy Spirit in my life, in Jesus' name.*
2. *Holy Spirit, overshadow me today and fill me with divine power, in Jesus' name.*
3. *Lord, remove every barrier that resists Your incubation in my life, in Jesus' name.*
4. *Holy Spirit, birth through me ideas, ministries, and miracles that glorify Christ, in Jesus' name.*
5. *I decree that the good things buried in me will manifest this year and bless multitudes, in Jesus' name.*

Wednesday 7 January   **FOCUS ON DIVINE DIRECTION**

Read: Psalm 32:6-11

Bible in 1 year: Prov. 22-24
Bible in 2 years: Gen. 13-14

"I will instruct you and teach you in the way you should go; I will guide you with My eye." (Psalm 32:8).

The promise of Enlargement in Isaiah 54:2 requires us not only to prepare the space but also to know where to stretch the tent cords. God is a strategic Father, and His desire is not for you to stumble, but to walk securely into your expanded future. This is why the central purpose of intimacy with God this month is to secure Divine Direction, which is the ability to receive and follow God's strategic instructions.

King David, in Psalm 32, testifies to the Lord's guidance: *"I will instruct you and teach you in the way you should go."* This is a personal promise. God doesn't just give general principles; He promises to guide you with His eye, a sign of intimate, moment-by-moment connection. This requires sensitivity on your part, which is precisely what prayer and fasting will cultivate in your spirit this season. When you are fasting, intentionally choose the voice of the Spirit over the clamor of the flesh and the world. He will show you great and mighty things which you don't know (Jeremiah 33:3).

To be enlarged without direction is like acquiring a ship without a rudder; you may have potential, but you will drift and crash. Many people rush into the new year, driven by excitement or human pressure, only to fall into error. The

Psalmist warns against being *"like the horse or like the mule, which have no understanding, which must be harnessed with bit and bridle"* (v. 9).

My prayer for you is that your prayer and fasting should serve as the "Bit and bridle," aligning your will to God's specific instruction. Today, realize that your greatest asset in the pursuit of enlargement is not your effort, but your ability to hear and obey the voice of your strategic guide – the Holy Spirit. Secure His direction, and your enlargement is guaranteed.

Action: *Today, dedicate at least five minutes of your prayer time to silence. Just listen to the Holy Spirit!*

Let us pray
1. *Father, thank You for the promise of instruction and guidance; I choose to follow Your path wholeheartedly this year, in Jesus' name.*
2. *Holy Spirit, sensitize my heart and sharpen my spiritual hearing to receive Your Divine Direction clearly, in Jesus' name.*
3. *I reject the spirit of confusion and the tendency to rush ahead of Your strategic plan for my enlargement, in Jesus' name.*
4. *Lord, reveal any area where I have been stubborn or operated without Your counsel, and grant me grace to repent, in Jesus' name.*
5. *As I seek intimacy through prayer and fasting, show me the specific 'way I should go' to manifest Your enlargement in my life, in Jesus' name.*

Thursday 8 January   **THE SINS OF SODOM**

Read: Ezekiel 16:46-50

> **Bible in 1 year:** Prov. 25-28
> **Bible in 2 years:** Gen. 15-16

"Now this was the sin of your sister Sodom: She and her daughters were arrogant, overfed and unconcerned; they did not help the poor and needy" (Ezekiel 16:49 NIV).

Sin always ends in destruction. Sodom's destruction was not only because of immorality but also because of arrogance and pride. Ezekiel 16:49 makes it clear: they were proud, prosperous, and careless about the needy. They enjoyed extraordinary grace and abundance, yet forgot the God who blessed them. Their arrogance blinded them to their sin until judgment fell.

"*Pride*" in Hebrew is '*Ga'own*', meaning "Arrogance, swelling, or self-exaltation." Pride is an inflated heart that forgets God and despises others.

History shows that pride often precedes downfall (Proverbs 16:18). Nations, families, and individuals that rise in wealth and knowledge usually begin to despise God and exalt themselves. For instance, in polygamous homes, children of the favored wife may grow up entitled, despising others, only to discover that arrogance opens the door to ruin. Pride creates a false sense of security that eventually collapses suddenly.

Jesus warns us, *"What do you benefit if you gain the whole world but lose your own soul?" (Mark 8:36).* Paul also asked,

"What do you have that you did not receive? And if you did receive it, why do you boast as though you did not?" (1 Corinthians 4:7). Everything we are and have is a gift of grace from God, not a reason to boast.

How then do we cultivate humility? Beloved, remember where God picked you from. Reflect on His mercy and how far He has carried you. Remember that blessings are given not to inflate us but to bless others (Genesis 12:2). Finally, remember that pride destroys, but humility attracts grace: *"God opposes the proud but gives grace to the humble" (James 4:6).*

Pride leads to destruction, but humility secures favor. Learn from Sodom—root out pride before it roots out your destiny.

Action: *Ask God to guide you on how you will invest part of the blessings He has given you to advance His mission this year. Write it down!*

Let us pray

1. *Father, thank You for Your mercy and blessings in my life, in Jesus' name.*
2. *Lord, deliver me from the sins of Sodom – pride, arrogance, and false security, in Jesus' name.*
3. *Father, teach me always to remember where You brought me from, in Jesus' name.*
4. *Father, help me to use every blessing to be a blessing to others this year, in Jesus' name.*
5. *Father, keep me humble and broken before You, that I may always enjoy Your grace, in Jesus' name.*

Friday 9 January   **ACTIVATE YOUR SPIRITUAL SENSES**

Read: John 5:19-23

> **Bible in 1 year:** Prov. 29-31
> **Bible in 2 years:** Gen. 17-18

"But solid food is for the mature, who by constant use have trained themselves to distinguish good from evil" (Hebrews 5:14 NIV).

Every believer has spiritual senses, just as the body has physical senses. Do you know that you can see, hear, feel, smell, and taste in the spirit? But for many Christians, these senses remain dormant because they have not trained themselves to use them. To walk effectively with God, you must awaken and sharpen your spiritual sensitivity through the Word, prayer, listening, and obeying the Holy Spirit.

The Greek word for "Trained" in Hebrews 5:14 is *'Gumnazo,'* meaning "To exercise or discipline." It's where we get the English word *gymnasium*. Just as athletes train their bodies for strength and skill, you must train your spirit to discern God's voice and perceive His presence. Spiritual sensitivity does not come by accident; it grows through intentional discipline and practice.

Interestingly, Jesus was perfectly sensitive to His Father's will. He said, *"The Son can do nothing by Himself; He can do only what He sees His Father doing" (John 5:19)*. In His Father's presence, He heard when to speak, saw where to go, and discerned people's hearts. His life was led by spiritual perception, not human reasoning.

Many believers miss divine direction because their spiritual senses are dull. When you ignore prayer, the Word, or fellowship with the Holy Spirit, you lose your ability to perceive divine signals. But when you spend time with Him, your inner eyes open to see God's plans, your ears hear His whispers, and your heart discerns His will.

Elisha's servant in 2 Kings 6:17 could only see danger until God opened his eyes to see divine protection. When your spiritual senses are active, you see victory even in adversity.

Action: *Spend quality time in prayer and the Word today – ask the Holy Spirit to activate your spiritual senses!*

Let us pray
1. *Lord, thank You for giving me spiritual senses to know and follow You, in Jesus' name.*
2. *Holy Spirit, sharpen my spiritual perception and help me discern Your voice clearly, in Jesus' name.*
3. *Lord, remove every spiritual dullness, distraction, or blindness from my life, in Jesus' name.*
4. *Father, train me daily through Your Word to distinguish good from evil, in Jesus' name.*
5. *I decree that because my spiritual senses are activated, I will not miss my way nor fall into the devil's trap, in Jesus' name.*

Saturday 10 January **TRAPPED BY FASTING?**

Read: 1 Samuel 14:24-30

Bible in 1 year: 1 Cor. 1-3
Bible in 2 years: Gen. 19

"Is not this the kind of fasting I have chosen: to loose the chains of injustice and untie the cords of the yoke, to set the oppressed free and break every yoke?" (Isaiah 58:6 NIV).

Fasting is a powerful spiritual discipline when rightly practiced, but it can also become a religious trap when done without discernment. True fasting is not about hunger strikes to impress God but about aligning our desires with His will.

Saul is an example of misapplied fasting. On a day when God had called Israel to battle, Saul imposed a fast on his army (1 Samuel 14:24-30). Instead of empowering them for victory, his religious command weakened the soldiers. The result was confusion, reduced strength, and even sin when the famished army ate meat with blood. Saul's action shows that fasting without God's direction can hinder rather than help. The Jews in Isaiah's day were trapped by the practice of fasting without righteousness. While they boasted about their fasts, they maltreated their servants, exploited the weak, and were idolatrous. Fasting should change us, making us consecrated disciples of Christ.

Today, how do people get trapped by fasting? Some impose their personal instruction on others, turning it into law. Others use fasting as a display of spirituality or as a qualification to earn God's favor. Some fast for every problem, ignoring wisdom, prayer, or action. Jesus warned against hypocritical fasting done to be seen by men (Matthew 6:16-18).

Acceptable fasting is Spirit-led, not man-driven. It must be guided by wisdom and humility. We do not twist God's hand with fasting; instead, we submit our will to His. When the early church fasted, it was in alignment with the Spirit's leading, and it brought clarity to the mission of Saul and Barnabas (Acts 13:2-3).

Years ago, a young man from my village fasted and died under a bridge in Douala because he didn't learn how to fast correctly. Fasting must never become a religious snare. It should align you with God's heart, empower you to pray effectively, and prepare you for His purposes.

Action: *Ask God to show you things you need to adjust in your life as you fast and pray for 2026!*

Let us pray
1. *Father, thank You for the gift of fasting as a means to draw closer to You, in Jesus' name.*
2. *Lord, deliver me from religious fasting that is void of Your Spirit, in Jesus' name.*
3. *Father, teach me to fast with wisdom and balance, in Jesus' name.*
4. *Father, let my fasting produce clarity, power, and freedom in Christ, in Jesus' name.*
5. *Father, restore my prayer life and deepen my communion with You throughout this year, in Jesus' name.*

Sunday 11 January **THE POWER OF VISION**

Read: Habakkuk 2:1-4

> **Bible in 1 year:** 1 Cor. 4-6
> **Bible in 2 years:** Gen. 20-21

"Then the LORD answered me and said: 'Write the vision and make it plain on tablets, that he may run who reads it'" (Habakkuk 2:2).

The prophet Habakkuk teaches us a critical lesson in securing the Divine Direction necessary for Enlargement: first, we must see it, and second, we must document it. The instruction to *"Write the vision and make it plain"* is the Lord's mandate for transforming a prophetic word into a practical, actionable blueprint. We cannot confidently stretch our tent cords (Isaiah 54:2) and run toward a future that remains hazy and undefined.

This January, as we engage in deep Intimacy through prayer and fasting, we are positioning ourselves on the watchtower, like Habakkuk, waiting for God's specific revelation. The vision you receive – the clear picture of your enlarged future is the fuel you need for the year. When you write it down, you affirm your faith and establish a tangible anchor for your spiritual stakes. The clarity of the written word empowers not just you, but also those who read it, creating shared momentum.

Proverbs 29:18 makes it clear that a lack of vision leads to stagnation. Many people enter the new year without a clear vision of where they are going spiritually, professionally, or economically. You cannot possess the promise of enlargement without a clear vision.

Conversely, a clear, God-given vision guides your prayers, justifies your fasting, and ensures that your hard work is purposeful. The vision provides the framework for your breakthrough to manifest, even if the timing seems delayed (v. 3).

Let your spiritual discipline this month yield clear, God-breathed instructions. When you possess the written blueprint, you possess the confidence to run and overcome every obstacle standing between you and your Enlargement this year.

I heard from God in October 2010, "Write a prayer guide to help my people pray." I went to work immediately, and by January 2011, we published the first Prayer Storm Daily Prayer Guide. Fifteen years later, the work has not died because the vision and the instruction were clear. A clear vision guarantees enlargement!

Action: *Write in your journal the desires, goals, and instructions concerning 2026 that you have received from God since the beginning of this month.*

Let us pray
1. *Father, I thank You for the spirit of revelation that grants me clear sight of my destiny, in Jesus' name.*
2. *Holy Spirit, anoint my mind and hands to accurately capture the specific, plain vision for my enlargement this year, in Jesus' name.*
3. *I declare that I possess the clarity of vision, and I will run with the Divine Direction I receive, in Jesus' name.*
4. *Lord, as I seek You in intimacy, let my written vision align perfectly with the expansive purpose of Isaiah 54, in Jesus' name.*

5. *I reject the spirit of stagnation; my life is moving forward and will manifest the enlarged blueprint I possess, in Jesus' name.*

Monday 12 January   **STAY WITH THE HOLY SPIRIT**

Read: John 16:12-15

Bible in 1 year: 1 Cor. 7-9
Bible in 2 years: Gen. 22-23

"When the Spirit of truth comes, He will guide you into all truth… He will glorify Me, because it is from Me that He will receive what He will make known to you" (John 16:13-14 NIV).

Do you desire to experience divine enlargement this year? You must learn to walk closely with the Holy Spirit. Jesus promised His disciples that when He returned to the Father, the Spirit would continue His work in them. The Spirit is not an idea or a force; He is the personal presence of Jesus within you. He teaches, guides, corrects, comforts, and empowers. Intimacy with Him is the engine of growth.

Paul lived this reality. He said, *"The fellowship of the Holy Spirit be with you all" (2 Corinthians 13:14)*. His ministry, courage, and revelation were not products of natural ability but of daily communion with the Spirit. Enlargement begins when you stop depending on your own wisdom and start yielding to the gentle whispers and rebukes of the Holy Spirit.

When I was considering getting married, I thought of a young sister in our youth group as the best choice. After sharing with my parents, who are believers, we agreed that she was good for me. But before I went to talk to the sister, the Holy Spirit warned me one early morning during my devotion, "Be careful. Don't go for her!" I dropped the idea and shared it with my parents. We prayed, and God led me to Anna. Before I got to her, she saw me in a trance during her prayer time, and the Holy Spirit told her, "This is your husband."

The Greek word *'Koinonia'* means "Fellowship" – deep partnership, participation, or sharing of life. It is not a casual conversation but a continuous exchange. The Holy Spirit reveals Christ, and you respond in obedience.

True enlargement happens when your spirit stays in *koinonia* with the Holy Spirit. The more you walk with the Holy Spirit, the larger your understanding, peace, and influence become.

Action: *Spend at least 10 minutes today just listening in silence – ask the Holy Spirit to speak, and write what you sense!*

Let us pray
1. *Father, thank You for sending the Holy Spirit to dwell and walk with me daily, in Jesus' name.*
2. *Holy Spirit, draw me into deeper fellowship and sensitivity to Your voice, in Jesus' name.*
3. *I break every hardness of heart that keeps me from recognizing Your leading, in Jesus' name.*
4. *Holy Spirit, teach me to rely on You in decisions, relationships, and ministry, in Jesus' name.*
5. *Father, enlarge my inner capacity to host Your presence and manifest Your power, in Jesus' name.*
6. *I decree that I will not lack strength, wisdom, and power to accomplish my destiny, in Jesus' name.*

Prophetic Prayers of the Week

1. **"Jabez called... and God granted his request." (1 Chronicles 4:10)** *My territory will expand abundantly this year, in Jesus' name.*
2. **"You will spread abroad." (Genesis 28:14)** *Nothing will stop my enlargement this year, in Jesus' name.*
3. **"It will not come near you." (Psalm 91:7)** *I am safe and secure from diseases, disaster, and death, in Jesus' name.*

Tuesday 13 January   **UNLOCKING THE TREASURES OF DARKNESS**

Read: Isaiah 45:1-5

Bible in 1 year: 1 Cor. 10-12
Bible in 2 years: Gen. 24

"I will give you the treasures of darkness and hidden riches of secret places, that you may know that I, the LORD, who call you by your name, Am the God of Israel." (Isaiah 45:3, NKJV).

The promise of Enlargement often brings questions of practical provision: *How will I fund the vision? Where will the resources come from to stretch the tent cords?* The answer lies in our January theme: Enlarged Through Intimacy. God promises to give us the *"Treasures of darkness and hidden riches of secret places."* These are not ordinary resources; they are supernatural provisions, divine ideas, and unique favour that are unavailable to the natural eye – they are unlocked through intimacy.

This declaration to Cyrus demonstrates God's ability to orchestrate political and economic events to provide for His people. The "Treasures of darkness" are the hidden wealth, unique investment strategies, or breakthrough ideas that only Divine Direction can reveal. This season of prayer and fasting is the spiritual key that unlocks these secret places. By denying the physical and elevating the spiritual, we sensitize ourselves to receive the specific, strategic counsel that leads to wealth creation and supernatural provision.

The purpose of this supernatural provision is clear: *"that you may know that I, the LORD… Am the God of Israel."* The enlargement must be traced back to Him, not to human genius or luck. When God unveils these hidden riches, your ability to "stretch out the curtains" (Isaiah 54:2) is achieved without strain or struggle.

Press in today, believing that your intimacy with God is currently positioning you to access the wealth stored in secret places for the manifestation of your destiny.

Action: *Identify one area of your life or ministry that requires significant financial or resource breakthrough for its enlargement. Spend 10 minutes specifically praying for the "treasures of darkness"—the unique idea or connection—to be revealed to you today.*

Let us pray

1. *Father, I thank You that You are the Revealer of secrets and the Giver of hidden riches, in Jesus' name.*
2. *Holy Spirit, release the Divine Direction and strategic ideas I need to access the supernatural provision for my enlargement, in Jesus' name.*
3. *I declare that every resource and capital necessary to stretch my tent cords is being supernaturally released in my favour, in Jesus' name.*
4. *Lord, let my fasting and prayer dismantle the veil over the hidden treasures reserved for my destiny, in Jesus' name.*
5. *I receive the wisdom and revelation that distinguishes me as one called by God, manifesting Your glory through supernatural provision, in Jesus' name.*

Wednesday 14 January   **BE A MAN OR WOMAN OF PEACE**

Read: Isaiah 11:3–9

> **Bible in 1 year:** 1 Cor. 13-16
> **Bible in 2 years:** Gen. 25-26

"Blessed are the peacemakers, for they will be called children of God" (Matthew 5:9).

Peace is one of the clearest marks of a true child of God. To be a man or woman of peace means to live and act like Jesus Christ, the *Prince of Peace* (Isaiah 9:6). Everywhere Jesus, the man of Peace went, He brought calm to storms, healing to broken lives, and reconciliation where there was division.

The prophecy of Isaiah in our text paints a beautiful picture of Jesus Christ, the coming Messiah, as the ultimate Man of Peace. It says, *"The wolf will live with the lamb, the leopard will lie down with the goat... and a little child will lead them"* (vs. 6). This is not just poetic imagery; it is a revelation of Christ's power to bring harmony where there is hostility.

The Hebrew word *'Shalom,'* means "Nothing missing, nothing broken." It describes a state where everything is restored to perfect divine order. Jesus came to bring *shalom* to humanity – peace between God and man, and peace within the human heart. Colossians 1:20 says, *"Through Him, God reconciled everything to Himself... making peace through the blood of His cross."*

In Isaiah's prophecy, the ferocious and the fragile coexist peacefully because the knowledge of the Lord fills the earth. When you let Christ rule in your heart, His peace will fill your home, your relationships, and your world.

Jesus is our Prince of Peace (Isaiah 9:6). His peace, *shalom,* is more than quietness; it means wholeness, completeness, harmony, and total well-being. Wherever Jesus reigns, chaos is replaced by calm, hatred by love, and confusion by divine order. When He meets a sinner, guilt and shame give way to forgiveness and reconciliation.

To be a man or woman of peace, you must let His Spirit transform you. The more you know Jesus, the more you become like Him – gentle, forgiving, and reconciliatory. Your presence should bring calm where there is tension and healing where there is hurt.

Action: *Is there someone you have not been getting along with well? Call the person this week or show them kindness in any way!*

Let us pray
1. *Father, thank You for sending Jesus, the Prince of Peace, into my life and family, in Jesus' name.*
2. *Father, fill me with the shalom of Christ – peace in my heart, mind, and relationships, in Jesus' name.*
3. *Lord, use me to bring reconciliation and healing wherever there is conflict, in Jesus' name.*
4. *Holy Spirit, teach me to walk daily in the peace that comes from trusting You, in Jesus' name.*
5. *I decree that the peace of Jesus Christ – shalom – will govern my life, my home, and my workplace, in Jesus' name.*

Thursday 15 January **PUT YOUR LIFE IN ORDER**

Read: Genesis 1:28-31

> **Bible in 1 year: 2 Cor. 1-3**
> **Bible in 2 years:** Gen. 27

"But everything should be done in a fitting and orderly way" (1 Corinthians 14:40 NIV).

God is a God of order. Creation itself reveals this truth – day followed night, seas had boundaries, and the sun and moon were set in their proper places (Genesis 1). Disorder, on the other hand, opens the door to chaos, confusion, and destruction. Paul reminded the Corinthians, *"But everything should be done in a fitting and orderly way" (1 Corinthians 14:40).* If you want peace and progress in life, you must put your life in order.

"*Order*" in Greek is *'Taxis'*, meaning "Arrangement, discipline, alignment, and proper sequence." Order is God's design for fruitfulness, multiplication, and peace.

First, order begins with light – the Word of God and prayer. Seek light daily to navigate life's darkness (Psalm 119:105). Speak God's Word to your mountains (Mark 11:23). Prioritize time for Bible reading and prayer. Without spiritual order, every other area of life suffers.

Second, order your family and relationships. Family is the most important unit apart from God. When the family is attacked, you become destabilized. Value healthy relationships, break away from toxic influences, and intentionally nurture connections. Even a simple call can strengthen bonds (Proverbs 17:17).

Third, order your finances and health. Financial disorder is the root of many problems – stress in marriages, instability in children, and even health issues. Putting God first with the tithe (Malachi 3:10), planning your money, avoiding unnecessary competition, impromptu spending, and living within your means are key. Save after honoring God. Live at your level; do not let sudden income inflate your lifestyle. Proverbs 21:20 says, *"The wise store up choice food and olive oil, but fools gulp theirs down."*

Like buttons on a shirt, if the first one is misplaced, the rest misalign. So, it is with life. If God is not first, nothing else aligns. But when order begins with Him, peace and fruitfulness follow.

Action: *Check your family and finances. Is everything well? Put things in order now!*

Let us pray
1. *Father, thank You for being a God of order and peace in my life, in Jesus' name.*
2. *Lord, help me put You first through prayer and the Word daily, in Jesus' name.*
3. *Father, restore order in my family and relationships; remove every attack of disunity, in Jesus' name.*
4. *Father, deliver me from financial disorder and give me wisdom to manage resources well, in Jesus' name.*
5. *Father, strengthen me to live with discipline, contentment, and purpose, in Jesus' name.*

Friday 16 January   **RESPONDING TO DIVINE REVELATION**

Read: Isaiah 6:1-8

Bible in 1 year: 2 Cor. 4-6
Bible in 2 years: Gen. 28-29

"Today, if you hear his voice, do not harden your hearts" (Hebrews 4:7 NIV).

When God reveals Himself to you, He does so to transform you. Divine revelation is not for your excitement or spiritual show; it is an invitation to become more like Christ. Paul understood this when he prayed for believers to receive *"the Spirit of wisdom and revelation" to know Christ better (Ephesians 1:17).*

The Greek word for "Revelation" is *'Apokalypsis,'* meaning "Unveiling" or "Disclosure." It refers to the removal of a veil that hides spiritual truth from the heart. When God gives revelation, He uncovers hidden realities about Himself, your condition, or His purpose for your life. Divine revelation is not new information; it is illumination. Hidden realities about your destiny are unveiled.

Isaiah's encounter with God in the temple is one of the clearest pictures of divine revelation. When the veil lifted, he saw the Lord in His glory and his own unworthiness. True revelation always brings repentance before it brings mission. Isaiah cried, *"Woe to me! I am ruined! For I am a man of unclean lips." (v.5).* Immediately, God sent a seraph to cleanse him.

Reflect on this touching testimony of a sister, a choir leader, who encountered the power of the Holy Spirit during a prayer meeting. God's Spirit revealed pride in her heart, and she broke down in tears and repented. That night marked the beginning of her powerful ministry to young women. Revelation revealed her sin, but also released her calling.

Friend, God reveals Himself not to condemn you, but to cleanse and commission you. Once Isaiah was purified, he heard God's call: *"Whom shall I send?"* and he answered, *"Here I am. Send me."* Every revelation demands a response. When God shows you His will, your duty is to say "Yes, Lord!"

Action: *Has God been telling you to do something? Respond today!*

Let us pray
1. *Lord, thank You for revealing Yourself and Your will to me, in Jesus' name.*
2. *Father, open my spiritual eyes to see what You are showing me, in Jesus' name.*
3. *Lord, purge me from every sin or attitude that blinds me to Your voice, in Jesus' name.*
4. *Father, give me courage to obey every divine instruction You reveal to me this year, in Jesus' name.*
5. *I decree that every revelation from God will lead to transformation and victory in my life, in Jesus' name.*

Saturday 17 January **DO NOT SPARE!**

Read: Joshua 1:5-9

> **Bible in 1 year:** 2 Cor. 7-9
> **Bible in 2 years:** Gen. 30

"Have I not commanded you? Be strong and of good courage; do not be afraid, nor be dismayed, for the LORD your God is with you wherever you go." (Joshua 1:9).

The prophetic mandate to "Enlarge the place of your tent" includes the bold instruction to *"do not spare" (Isaiah 54:2)*. This means holding nothing back – no hesitation, no fear, and no settling for smallness in your vision for 2026. Once you secure Divine Direction in the place of Intimacy, the corresponding requirement is the spiritual courage to execute your God-given plan.

Joshua, standing at the door of the Promised Land, received this triple command: *"Be strong and of good courage; do not be afraid, nor be dismayed" (Joshua 1:9)*. This is the language of warfare against doubt and the negative voices of the enemy of your destiny. Friend, are you aware that fear is the spiritual enemy that paralyzes action and aborts enlargement?

Throughout his life, Joshua courageously confronted the nations that occupied the Promised Land and possessed his God-given possession. The only foundation for this kind of boldness and audacity demonstrated by Joshua is the assurance that we are not moving alone: *"for the LORD your God is with you wherever you go" (v. 9)*. Our prayer and fasting this month have secured this covenant of presence. You are not alone! God's anointing is upon you!

The "Do not spare" mandate requires you to break free from the spirit of scarcity, past failures, or self-doubt. It's a call to think bigger, pray wider, and launch higher than ever before. You have surely received a blueprint from the Holy Spirit. It is time to step out with the faith that commands mountains to move. Whatever your hands find to do, do it with all your heart and strength, and you will experience divine expansion in Jesus' name.

Action: *Identify one area in your life where you have been holding back due to fear. Throughout today, declare by faith your victory over that fear and what you will do.*

Let us pray
1. *Father, thank You for the spirit of power and courage within me, in Jesus' name.*
2. *Holy Spirit, release boldness on me to act on the Divine Direction received, in Jesus' name.*
3. *I declare that I will not spare in my prayers, efforts, and faith this year, in Jesus' name.*
4. *I renounce every spirit of fear, timidity, and discouragement, in Jesus' name.*
5. *Lord, may my bold obedience manifest the full measure of my promised enlargement, in Jesus' name.*

Sunday 18 January **WHEN GOD WANTS TO DESTROY A MAN**

Read: 1 Samuel 15:17-23

Bible in 1 year: 2 Cor. 10-13
Bible in 2 years: Gen. 31

"Pride goes before destruction, and a haughty spirit before a fall" (Proverbs 16:18).

God never delights in the destruction of anyone. Scripture says, *"As surely as I live… I take no pleasure in the death of the wicked, but rather that they turn from their ways and live" (Ezekiel 33:11)*. Yet, when a person hardens his heart and rejects God repeatedly, certain signs reveal the path to destruction.

First, God withdraws light. Spiritual blindness sets in. Without discernment, the person makes choices that lead to ruin (Romans 1:21). Samson ignored warning signs until his eyes were literally gouged out (Judges 16:21).

Second, he becomes conceited, always spotting faults in others while ignoring his own. Jesus warned of the hypocrisy of seeing the speck in another's eye while ignoring the plank in one's own (Matthew 7:3-5).

Third, arrogance and greed take root. Nebuchadnezzar boasted of his kingdom, but God humbled him until he acknowledged Heaven's rule (Daniel 4:30-37). Greed blinded Judas, who betrayed Christ for silver, ending in tragedy (Matthew 27:3-5).

Fourth, such a person begins making illogical mistakes. King Saul, once chosen by God, made rash vows, disobeyed divine instructions, and rejected Samuel's counsel, ultimately losing the kingdom (1 Samuel 15:22-23). Rejecting wise counsel is a sure sign of imminent downfall.

Finally, destruction follows. Proverbs 29:1 warns, *"He who is often reproved, yet stiffens his neck, will suddenly be broken beyond healing."*

But there is hope: repentance can reverse the course. The Ninevites were destined for destruction, but when they humbled themselves in fasting and prayer, God relented (Jonah 3:10).

Examine your life today. If you see these signs, run back to God. His mercy still speaks louder than judgment.

Action: *Wait quietly before God today and ask Him to expose any hidden rebellion in your heart you need to deal with.*

Let us pray

1. *Father, thank You for warning me in love before destruction, in Jesus' name.*
2. *Lord, restore my spiritual sight and discernment, in Jesus' name.*
3. *Father, deliver me from pride, arrogance, and conceit, in Jesus' name.*
4. *Dear Father, uproot greed and selfishness from my heart, in Jesus' name.*
5. *Father, deliver me from the path of destruction and order my steps this year, in Jesus' name.*

Monday 19 January **ENLARGED THROUGH SUFFERING**

Read: Philippians 3:10-11

> **Bible in 1 year:** 1 Sam. 1-3
> **Bible in 2 years:** Gen. 32-33

"That I may know Him and the power of His resurrection, and the fellowship of His sufferings, being made conformable unto His death" (Philippians 3:10 KJV).

Many people want to know Christ's power, but few are willing to share in His suffering. Yet suffering is often the classroom where intimacy with God grows deepest. Paul understood that pain was not punishment; it was partnership. Every tear he shed for the Gospel deepened his fellowship with Christ.

Jesus Himself was *"A man of sorrows and acquainted with grief" (Isaiah 53:3)*. In Gethsemane, He wrestled with anguish. Yet, He still said, *"Not my will but yours be done" (Luke 22:42)*. His obedience through suffering brought the most significant enlargement – salvation for all mankind. When you walk through pain with God, you don't just endure it; you are transformed by it. Are you going through pain? Is it transforming or deforming you?

Joseph's story is another clear picture. Betrayed by his brothers, imprisoned unjustly, and forgotten by men, Joseph could have grown bitter. But through his trials, he learned to trust God's presence more than his position. When he finally rose to power, he said, *"God turned it for good."*

(Genesis 50:20). The prison prepared him for the palace. Unfortunately, pain has destroyed some people.

The Greek word *'Koinonia'* in this context means "Sharing deeply in another's experience." Paul didn't want to merely observe Christ's suffering; he wanted to share it, knowing that through it, he would also share Christ's resurrection power. Intimacy grows when you meet God not only in blessings, but also in battles.

Your suffering may be painful, but it is not purposeless – it makes you spiritually powerful. God enlarges your heart through what you endure, so that you can later comfort and strengthen others (2 Corinthians 1:3-4).

Action: *Instead of asking "Why me…,?" Pray, "What are You teaching me, Lord?" — And write what He shows you!*

Let us pray

1. *Thank You, Lord, for being with me in every trial and turning my pain into purpose, in Jesus' name.*
2. *Lord, help me to see suffering as a place of fellowship, not abandonment, in Jesus' name.*
3. *Father, heal every wound in my heart and strengthen my faith through trials, in Jesus' name.*
4. *Father, let my present struggles produce wisdom, compassion, and endurance, in Jesus' name.*
5. *I decree that my pain shall produce glory – I will rise stronger, wiser, and more intimate with God, in Jesus' name.*

Prophetic Prayers of the Week

1. **"Draw near to God…" (James 4:8)** *My heart will draw closer to God daily, in Jesus' name.*

2. ***"My presence will go with you." (Exodus 33:14)*** *I will not wander away from God's presence, in Jesus' name.*
3. ***"As the deer pants…" (Psalm 42:1)*** *Nothing will quench my thirst for God this year, in Jesus' name.*

Tuesday 20 January   **ENLARGED THROUGH BROKENNESS**

Read: Luke 7:36- 50

Bible in 1 year: 1 Sam. 4-7
Bible in 2 years: Gen. 34-35

"Then she knelt behind him at his feet weeping. Her tears fell on his feet, and she wiped them off with her hair. Then she kept kissing his feet and putting perfume on them" (Luke 7:38 NLT).

Brokenness is the gateway to intimacy. It's not weakness; it's openness and spiritual vulnerability for deeper experiences with God. A broken heart is a fertile ground for the work of the Holy Spirit. Is your heart broken or hardened?

In Simon's house, a sinful woman came to Jesus carrying an alabaster jar. She didn't say much, yet her tears spoke more loudly than words. While others judged her, Jesus saw a heart completely yielded. He said, *"Her sins, which are many, are forgiven – for she loved much" (vs. 47)*. Her brokenness became the fragrance of intimacy.

I was born again on 7th February 1992. It was an awesome experience – my heart was overwhelmed with joy and peace as I received the forgiveness of sins from the Lord. Unfortunately, later that year, I fell back into sin and abandoned the faith because I didn't separate from my unbelieving friends. In August 1993, I had a second encounter with Jesus Christ. The conviction was so profound that I wept for over three hours, repenting of my sins. My heart literally melted inside, and my life changed forever. I have never gone back again. I have been moving from glory to glory, by God's grace.

In Luke 7:38, "Weep" is the Greek word *'Klaio,'* which means "To wail from deep pain but with hope of relief." God never despises *Klaio;* He transforms it into healing and expansion. That is what He did to me in August 1993. I have witnessed many repent in sincere tears and how God transformed their lives.

Today, many want enlargement without surrender. But before God enlarges your influence, He first breaks your pride. The perfume could not fill the room until the jar was broken. Likewise, the Holy Spirit cannot fully flow through a hardened heart. When you pour yourself out before Jesus – your pain, mistakes, and fears, He fills those empty spaces with His love and power.

Brokenness invites God's fullness. The place of your tears can become the place of your testimony.

Action: *Pour out your heart honestly before God today—don't hide your pain; surrender it!*

Let us pray
1. *Father, thank You because You draw near to the brokenhearted and You heal our wounds, in Jesus' name.*
2. *Father, break every pride and hardness in me that hinders intimacy, in Jesus' name.*
3. *O Lord, turn every pain and failure in my life into an instrument of Your glory, in Jesus' name.*
4. *Father, enlarge my capacity to love and forgive through the power of brokenness, in Jesus' name.*

5. *Place your hand on your chest and pray 5 times, "I receive divine healing in my body, soul, and spirit now, in Jesus' name.*

Wednesday 21 January **SEEK HIS FACE, NOT JUST HIS HAND**

Read: Psalm 27:4-14

> **Bible in 1 year:** 1 Sam. 8-10
> **Bible in 2 years:** Gen. 36

"When You said, "Seek My face," My heart said to You, "Your face, LORD, I will seek" (Psalm 27:8).

As we approach the latter half of this month focused on Enlargement Through Intimacy, we must check the motivation behind our pursuit. Have we been seeking God merely for His Hand (Direction, provision, blessing) or for His Face (His presence, love, and intimate knowledge)?

In our text, David reveals the heart of true devotion: when God called him to seek His face, his heart readily agreed. This is the goal of our January emphasis. Our focus is not only to receive things from God, we want Him. It is sad that some people are only interested in receiving miracles and not in resembling Jesus Christ, the miracle worker.

The promise of Enlargement (Isaiah 54:2) is not just about expanding space; it's about expanding our relationship with the Giver of the space. David testified that his greatest desire was to *"dwell in the house of the LORD all the days of my life" (v. 4).* This posture of seeking God's constant presence – His Face, is what qualifies us for safety and breakthrough. When we prioritize Him, the blessings of His hand – the favour, the Divine Direction, and the provision, follow effortlessly.

Fasting and prayer, at its purest, is an act of adoration, showing God that we value His person more than His gifts. If we only seek His gifts, we risk receiving the direction but lacking the spiritual stamina to sustain the enlargement. However, when we secure His face, we dwell in a place of supernatural rest, free from fear (v. 5).

Let today be a day of recalibration. Shift your focus from the pressures of your needs to the privilege of His presence. Your destiny is secured when your heart says, "Your face, Lord, I will seek."

Action: *Before you begin any prayer or study today, spend 10 minutes deliberately praising God, thanking Him for who He is (His attributes) rather than what He does (His blessings)!*

Let us pray
1. *Father, I thank You that You are a God who desires deep, genuine intimacy with me, in Jesus' name.*
2. *Holy Spirit, redirect my focus from seeking only Your blessings to passionately seeking Your glorious Face, in Jesus' name.*
3. *I declare that my heart's greatest desire is to dwell in Your presence and behold Your beauty forever, in Jesus' name.*
4. *Lord, as I prioritize intimacy with You, let the blessings of Your Hand—Direction and Enlargement—follow me automatically, in Jesus' name.*
5. *I reject the spirit of performance; I will rest in Your love, knowing that Your Presence is my ultimate assurance, in Jesus' name.*

Thursday 22 January   **FORGET THE SHAMEFUL PAST**

Read: Philippians 3:12-16

> **Bible in 1 year:** 1 Sam. 11-13
> **Bible in 2 years:** Gen. 37

"Brethren, I do not count myself to have apprehended; but one thing I do, forgetting those things which are behind and reaching forward to those things which are ahead, I press toward the goal for the prize of the upward call of God in Christ Jesus." (Philippians 3:13-14).

The command to "Enlarge the place of your tent" comes with a spiritual prerequisite: we must willingly discard the baggage of the past. Isaiah 54:4 explicitly instructs us to *"forget the shame of your youth, and the reproach of your widowhood you will remember no more."* Your past hurts, failures, and even old, celebrated successes, can become evil spiritual weights or roadblocks that prevent you from moving forward into the vast territory of your promised Enlargement this year.

The Apostle Paul understood that breakthrough requires relentless forward motion. Friend, if you back off, you will never break through! Paul made a conscious, daily decision to forget the things behind him – his past failures and successes. He excelled in ministry and finished his race gloriously (2 Timothy 4:7-8). You can experience great breakthrough this year.

However, you must know that you cannot run effectively toward the prize if you keep looking backward.

Do this exercise. Try to look up and down at the same time. Try walking forward while looking backward. It is impossible! It is strenuous!

If you want your intimacy with God to yield clear Divine Direction, you must turn off your mind from those past experiences that cloud your vision. Shame binds; unforgiveness slows you down; and focusing on past failures breeds fear.

Fasting and prayer are the spiritual tools that help us surrender our past baggage. They elevate our perspective, allowing us to see the immense value of the future prize – the upward call of God, which far outweighs the pain of the past.

You must actively choose to let go of every negative emotional weight and refuse to let the enemy use your dark history to disqualify your future. Today, align your heart with the mandate of God: your history does not dictate your destiny.

Action: *Take a moment to write down any specific shame, past failure, or unforgiveness you have been carrying that you must eliminate. Deal with them now!*

Let us pray
1. *Father, I thank You that in Christ, my past is forgiven and forgotten, in Jesus' name.*
2. *Holy Spirit, release the grace to willingly and completely let go of all shame, hurt, and failure that seeks to cling to me, in Jesus' name.*
3. *I declare that my history does not define me, but by the glorious, Enlarged future You have ordained for me, in Jesus' name.*

4. *Lord, give me a single focus to press toward the high calling of the prize, in Jesus' name.*
5. *I receive emotional and spiritual healing from every reproach of the past and step into my Divine Direction with renewed purpose, in Jesus' name.*

Friday 23 January   **WASHED IN MILK**

Read: 1 Peter 2:1-3

Bible in 1 year: 1 Sam. 14-16
Bible in 2 years: Gen. 38-39

"His eyes are like doves by the water streams, washed in milk, mounted like jewels" (Song of Solomon 5:12).

Jesus Christ died for us so we could be united with Him and share in His purity.

The Song of Solomon gives us one of the most tender images of Christ, our Bridegroom: *"His eyes are like doves ... washed in milk."* In Hebrew, the word *'Rahats'* means to wash, cleanse, or make bright. Milk, *'halav'* symbolizes nourishment, purity, and abundance. Together, the phrase *"washed in milk"* paints a picture of eyes full of purity, gentleness, and radiant clarity.

When Christ looks at His Bride, He does not see condemnation or corruption. His gaze is pure and compassionate, like eyes bathed in milk. The rabbis saw this as the purity of God's Word. Early Christian writers like Gregory of Nyssa saw it as the clarity of the Gospels. Both highlight a central truth: the eyes of Christ are full of light, and those who look into His gaze are nourished and cleansed.

Think of how a newborn baby thrives on pure milk (1 Peter 2:2). Just as milk sustains physical life, the Word of Christ sustains our spiritual life. His eyes, "Washed in milk," remind us that the Lord's perspective is always pure, abundant, and life-giving. He calls us to share that same vision – to see others with purity, mercy, and love.

A missionary testified how her view of a hostile tribe changed after weeks of prayer. Instead of seeing violent rebels, she began to see broken souls loved by Christ. That shift opened the door for salvation, reconciliation, and revival.

When our eyes are washed in the "Milk" of God's Word, we begin to see as He sees. Today, go before God in sincere prayer and ask Him to wash your eyes with the milk of His holy Word.

Action: *Establish a Bible reading program and ask God for the grace to follow it.*

Let us pray
1. *Father, thank You, Lord, for looking at me with eyes of purity and compassion, in Jesus' name.*
2. *Father, wash my eyes with the milk of Your Word so I may see clearly, in Jesus' name.*
3. *O Lord, deliver me from clouded vision caused by sin or corruption, in Jesus' name.*
4. *Father, help me to see others with love, mercy, and truth, in Jesus' name.*
5. *Let my life shine with the purity of Your gaze, in Jesus' name.*
6. *I declare that I will see uncommon visions in this season for uncommon results, in Jesus' name.*

Saturday 24 January   **PERFUMED WITH MYRRH**

Read: Song of Solomon 1:13; John 19:39

Bible in 1 year: 1 Sam. 17-20
Bible in 2 years: Gen. 40-41:1-36

"My beloved is to me a sachet of myrrh resting between my breasts" (Song of Solomon 1:13).

Jesus wants you to become all that He is. Naturally, every bridegroom wants the best for his bride. Do you know that you are Jesus' bride?

In our reading, the Bride describes her Beloved as *"A sachet of myrrh."* Myrrh, *'Mor'* in Hebrew, carries deep symbolic meaning in Scripture. It comes from a resin that must be crushed to release its fragrance. The word means "Bitterness," reminding us of suffering and sacrifice. In biblical times, myrrh was used for anointing, burial, and worship (Exodus 30:23; John 19:39).

This imagery beautifully points to Christ. At His birth, the wise men offered Him myrrh (Matthew 2:11), foreshadowing His sacrificial death on the cross. At His burial, Nicodemus brought myrrh to prepare His body (John 19:39). The sachet of myrrh symbolizes Jesus' presence, resting close to the heart of the believer and releasing the fragrance of His love and sacrifice.

To be "Perfumed with myrrh" is to carry the sweetness of Christ's suffering within us. It is important to remember that intimacy with Him is costly. Just as myrrh had to be crushed, so too our Lord was crushed for our salvation (Isaiah 53:5). Yet, out of His pain flows the aroma of eternal life.

A missionary once described living among persecuted believers who had lost everything yet radiated joy. Their fragrance was unmistakably the presence of Christ in suffering. Like the sachet of myrrh, they carried Jesus close to their hearts, and His beauty was evident to all.

The call for us today is to embrace both the sweetness and the cost of Christ's presence. To love Him is to share in His sufferings (Philippians 3:10), but it is also to radiate His fragrance everywhere we go (2 Corinthians 2:15).

Declaration: *Whatever the devil has prepared to steal my joy will not work!*

Let us pray
1. *Father, thank You for the fragrance of Your sacrificial love, in Jesus' name.*
2. *O Father, let my heart treasure Christ above all else, in Jesus' name.*
3. *Father, teach me to embrace the cost of intimacy with You, in Jesus' name.*
4. *Father, may my life radiate the fragrance of Christ to others everywhere I go, in Jesus' name.*
5. *Father, crush every pride and sin in me until Christ's aroma flows out, in Jesus' name.*

Sunday 25 January   **DESTROY THE VEIL OF PRIDE**

Read: Revelation 3:14-22

Bible in 1 year: Eph. 1-3
Bible in 2 years: Gen. 41:37-57; 42

"You say, 'I am rich; I have acquired wealth and do not need a thing.' But you do not realize that you are wretched, pitiful, poor, blind and naked" (Revelation 3:17).

Pride is one of the most subtle and dangerous spiritual veils you must destroy in your life. The veil of pride blinded the Laodicean believers. They believed they were spiritually strong because they were materially successful. But Jesus revealed the tragic truth: they were blind.

The Greek word for pride in Scripture is *'Huperephanos'*, meaning "To be lifted above measure, to exalt oneself, to feel superior or self-sufficient." It describes a person who rises above the place God intends for them. Pride removes your dependence on God and builds confidence in the flesh. Pride blinds you to your weaknesses, blinds you to your need for God, and blinds you to the corrections of the Holy Spirit. As long as pride occupies the heart, enlargement is impossible.

James 4:6 says, *"God resists the proud but gives grace to the humble."*
The word "Resists" literally means "To stand against." Why? God resists the proud because pride is a self-centered attitude that puts the person in a position of competing with

God for supremacy, making them unreceptive to divine grace and guidance.

Imagine yourself walking in a dark room with a candle in your hand. The candle represents God's guidance. Pride is like covering the candle with a clay pot – there is still light inside, but you cannot see it. You stumble, bump into furniture, and hurt yourself. The problem is not the absence of light; it is the presence of a covering. When you lift the pot, the whole room becomes bright. In the same way, when you remove pride, God's light floods your heart, bringing clarity, healing, and direction.

Divine enlargement requires humility. God can lift only those who bow before Him. Pride says, "I know enough." Humility says, "Lord, teach me." Pride says, "I don't need help." Humility says, "Without You, I am nothing."

Action: *Identify an area of your life where pride may be hiding and intentionally submit it to God!*

Let us pray

1. *Father, thank You for calling me to humility and dependence on You, in Jesus' name.*
2. *Lord, expose and break every hidden pride in my heart, in Jesus' name.*
3. *Father, give me grace to submit to Your Word and Your correction, in Jesus' name.*
4. *Lord, clothe me with the humility of Christ daily, in Jesus' name.*
5. *I decree that pride will not block my enlargement this year, in Jesus' name.*

Monday 26 January   **DON'T EAT YOUR SEED**

Read: Genesis 1:11-12, 8:22

Bible in 1 year: Eph. 4-6
Bible in 2 years: Gen. 43-44

"He gives seed to the sower and bread to the eater" (2 Corinthians 9:10).

Don't eat your seed; sow it for a great harvest!

Have you ever stopped to ask yourself *why* God put a seed inside the pear fruit? It is not for decoration. It is not accidental. It is divine wisdom hiding in plain sight. As I reflected on this question, I discovered many reasons – but at the heart of them all is God's economic principle: the seed principle. From the beginning, God designed everything in creation to multiply. Every fruit has a seed because God never intended life to end with one generation. A pear today holds in its center the possibility of an orchard tomorrow.

Likewise, everything God gives you carries a seed. Every salary, every small income, every gift, every skill, and every opportunity has a seed for your future hidden inside it. The tragedy for many believers is that they eat the entire fruit – including the seed, leaving nothing to plant for tomorrow. God gives *"Seed to the sower and bread to the eater."* Bread is for eating now; seed is for sowing. Wisdom is the ability to discern the difference – the capacity to separate what you must sow from your income.

To walk in financial freedom, Scripture gives us three practical steps. First is financial planning. *"The plans of the diligent lead surely to abundance" (Proverbs 21:5).* God Himself planned creation before He spoke it into being. Without a plan, money leaks away. Even your savings or *njangi* contributions must have a clear purpose.

Second is discipline. Proverbs 6 urges us to observe the ant. They are hardworking, consistent, and farsighted. Discipline means practicing self-control even when emotions disagree. Without discipline, financial freedom is impossible.

Third is **investment**. *"Invest in seven ventures, yes, in eight…" (Ecclesiastes 11:2).* Money grows only when it is deployed. Do not depend on one income stream. Let your money work for you.

Action: *Do you pay your tithes to God? If not, decide now to start doing it and pray for grace!*

Let us pray
1. *Father, thank You for blessing me with seeds continuously, in Jesus' name.*
2. *Lord, give me the wisdom to recognize the seed hidden in every income, gift, and opportunity You provide, in Jesus' name.*
3. *Father, deliver me from consuming my seed and teach me to distinguish clearly between bread for today and seed for tomorrow, in Jesus' name.*
4. *Holy Spirit, help me plan my finances with diligence, purpose, and godly wisdom, in Jesus' name.*
5. *Lord, grant me the discipline and self-control to work hard, avoid waste, and manage every resource faithfully, in Jesus' name.*
6. *Father, guide me into wise investments and multiple streams of income that honor You and secure my future, in Jesus' name.*

Prophetic Prayers of the Week
1. **"Abide in Me…" (John 15:4)** *I am unmovable, unbreakable, and unshakeable in Jesus Christ, in Jesus' name.*
2. **"He reveals His secrets to His servants." (Amos 3:7)** *I receive divine secrets and insights today, in Jesus' name.*
3. **"Be holy, for I am holy." (1 Peter 1:16)** *I walk in purity and holiness by God's power, in Jesus' name.*

Tuesday 27 January **SEVEN LAWS OF MAKING MONEY**

Read: Deuteronomy 8:1-18

> **Bible in 1 year:** Phil. 1-4
> **Bible in 2 years:** Gen. 45-46

"As a man thinks in his heart, so is he" (Proverbs 23:7).

God is not against you prospering; He is against greed and dishonesty. In fact, your prosperity in the covenant honors God (Vs. 18). Throughout Scripture, God reveals principles that govern financial increase. The underlying truth you must learn is that wealth is never accidental; it is the product of divine laws applied consistently.

1. ***The law of BELIEF:*** Scripture teaches, *"As a man thinks... so is he."* Poverty begins in the mind before it shows in the pocket. When you believe that you are called to prosper for God's glory (3 John 2), your actions begin to align with God's plan.
2. ***The law of FINANCIAL EDUCATION:*** Ignorance is costly. Lindon Johnson said, "Poverty has many roots, but ignorance is the taproot." Proverbs 24:3-4 says wealth is built through wisdom, understanding, and knowledge. You must learn about budgeting, saving, investment, and stewardship. Read, ask questions, attend seminars, and seek mentorship.
3. ***The law of RELATIONSHIPS:*** No destiny rises in isolation. Joseph met Pharaoh because of the cupbearer. David became king through Jonathan's loyalty. Proverbs 13:20 shows that association influences elevation.

Cultivate relationships intentionally. Walk with people who can help you succeed.

4. ***The law of CREATIVITY:*** God gives power to create wealth (Deuteronomy 8:18). God gives the power, and you create the wealth. Creativity is divine currency. Every problem hides an opportunity. Wealth flows to those who think differently and add value.

5. ***The law of EXCELLENCE:*** Daniel was promoted because an excellent spirit distinguished him (Daniel 6:3). Excellence speaks louder than connections. Whatever you do, do it well (Colossians 3:23-24).

6. ***The law of the ANOINTING:*** The Holy Spirit gives ideas, wisdom, and favor that no book can teach (Isaiah 45:3; 1 Samuel 16:13). Financial success is smoother when you partner with Him.

7. ***The law of the FARMER:*** God established sowing and reaping (Genesis 8:22). Give, and it shall be given (Luke 6:38). Invest in a business, and your finances will multiply. Farmers understand patience – seed, time, and harvest. Money does not come by prayer; it comes through strategic investment.

Action: *Today, ask God to show you the reason why you have stagnated financially!*

Let us pray

1. *Father, I thank You for giving me wisdom, principles, and the power to create wealth, in Jesus' name.*
2. *Lord, renew my mind and break every limiting belief that has kept me financially stagnant, in Jesus' name.*
3. *Holy Spirit, teach me wisdom, discipline, and understanding in managing money and building wealth, in Jesus' name.*

4. *Father, connect me to the right relationships, ideas, opportunities, and environments that lead to financial increase, in Jesus' name.*
5. *I decree that wealth, favor, creativity, and divine opportunities are locating me and my household from this day forward, in Jesus' name.*

Wednesday 28 January   **FIVE WAYS TO START A PETIT BUSINESS**

Read: Genesis 26:12-14

Bible in 1 year: Deut. 1-3
Bible in 2 years: Gen. 47-48

"The works of his hands shall be blessed" (Deuteronomy 28:12).

God delights in the prosperity of economic enlargement of His people. But prosperity moves in the direction of action, not wishful thinking. Many believers desire financial breakthroughs yet remain idle, waiting for a miracle, when God expects them to take responsibility.

Scripture teaches, *"If anyone is not willing to work, neither should he eat" (2 Thessalonians 3:10).* Starting a small business, no matter how little, is one of the simplest ways to activate God's blessing over the work of your hands.

1. ***Principle no. 1: PRODUCE:*** Be productive. Grow something, rear something, or make something. Every product begins with raw effort. When you produce, you create value that others are willing to pay for.
2. ***Principle no. 2: PROCESS:*** Do not stop at raw production; add value. When you turn maize into flour, cassava into garri, cocoa into powder, or plantains into chips, you increase your profit margin. Value addition is kingdom wisdom. Jesus turned water into wine, not to impress, but to improve value.

3. ***Principle no. 3: PRESERVE:*** The wisdom God gave Joseph saved an entire nation (Genesis 41:35-36). Preservation allows you to buy during abundance or low cost and sell during scarcity at higher returns. The wise do not waste opportunities; they store and prepare.
4. ***Principle no. 4: PACKAGE:*** Presentation determines perception. Packaging attracts customers before quality convinces them. Repackaging bulk items into retail units or improving branding can multiply sales. Even the anointing oil in Scripture was placed in a container. God values order and presentation.
5. ***Principle no. 5: PARTNERSHIP:*** Two are better than one (Ecclesiastes 4:9-10). Partnerships increase capital, multiply ideas, and distribute risks. When believers collaborate with integrity, capacity expands.

In the year of famine Isaac started producing food by digging wells to water his farms. He prospered through wisdom and hard work.

Action: *Choose one of the five principles and take a concrete step this week to start or improve a petit business.*

Let us pray
1. *Father, I thank You for giving me strength, ideas, and opportunities to work and prosper, in Jesus' name.*
2. *Lord, empower my hands to produce, create, and add value wherever I begin, in Jesus' name.*
3. *Holy Spirit, give me wisdom to preserve resources, plan ahead, and maximize every opportunity, in Jesus' name.*
4. *Father, help me package my products with excellence and connect me with the right partners for growth, in Jesus' name.*

5. *I decree that the works of my hands shall prosper and every small beginning in my life shall grow into abundance, in Jesus' name.*

Thursday 29 January **ACCELERATING IN FAVOUR**

Read: Luke 2:40-52

> **Bible in 1 year:** Deut. 4-6
> **Bible in 2 years:** Gen. 49-50

"And Jesus increased in wisdom and stature, and in favor with God and men." (Luke 2:52, NKJV).

The life of Jesus provides the ultimate blueprint for the process of Enlargement. His growth was defined by an increase in wisdom (a form of Divine Direction) and, crucially, by favour with God and men.

Favour is the supernatural accelerant that will empower you to move from possibility to undeniable reality with speed and ease. Favour is not earned; it is the spiritual consequence of intimacy and alignment with God. When we prioritize spending time daily with God, obeying His instructions, and walking in integrity, we gain His favor, which automatically translates into favor with people.

Proverbs 3:3-4 gives us the key to favor: *"Let not steadfast love and faithfulness forsake you; bind them around your neck; write them on the tablet of your heart. So you will find favor and good success in the sight of God and man."* The key is: (1) Steadfast love for God and people. (2) Faithfulness in all you do. (3) Walking in sincerity and integrity. Some people complain that they experience rejection wherever they go. Things will change if you apply these three keys everywhere you go.

Favor is divine approval. It causes human systems and individuals to work in your interest, opening doors that opposition tried to shut and providing resources that money cannot buy. Favor makes the complex simple and the difficult easy. Favor moves hearts to help you.

As we conclude this month of dedication, we must understand that God's favor seals the Divine Direction and impartation you have received. The direction God has given you will lead you to people and places where favor is already waiting. This is the ultimate distinguishing mark of the Christian life.

Reject the mentality of struggle; embrace the reality of grace. By walking in the wisdom and obedience gained in intimacy, you position yourself to receive the relentless favor that accelerates your Enlargement beyond the capacity of your natural effort.

Action: *Declare this throughout today: "I am a child of grace. I will enjoy favor with God and men everywhere I go this year, in Jesus' name."*

Let us pray
1. *Father, I thank You that I am highly favored, both by You and by man, in Jesus' name.*
2. *Holy Spirit, release the supernatural favor that removes every obstacle and opens every necessary door for my Enlargement, in Jesus' name.*
3. *I declare that as I walk in Your Divine Direction, favor will distinguish me in the marketplace and the Kingdom, in Jesus' name.*
4. *Lord, let favor bring the right connections and resources to help me stretch my tent cords effortlessly, in Jesus' name.*
5. *I receive the accelerating power of God's favor to quickly occupy my expansive territory in 2026, in Jesus' name.*

Friday 30 January   **ENJOYING SPIRITUAL IMMUNITY**

Read: Isaiah 54:11-17

> **Bible in 1 year:** Deut. 7-9
> **Bible in 2 years:** Matt. 1-2

"No weapon formed against you shall prosper, and every tongue which rises against you in judgment you shall condemn. This is the heritage of the servants of the LORD, and their righteousness is from Me," says the LORD" (Isaiah 54:17).

Today, we stand on the ultimate, glorious promise of the Enlargement mandate. Having spent the month securing Divine Direction through Intimacy, we are now ready to claim the ultimate assurance: SPIRITUAL IMMUNITY. God's vision for our enlarged territory (Isaiah 54:2) is not vulnerable; it is established in righteousness and protected by divine decree.

The promise of *"No weapon formed against you shall prosper" (v. 17),* is not a universal declaration; it is the heritage of the servants of the LORD – those who walk in the integrity of the covenant. The passage clarifies that this immunity is rooted in being established in righteousness (v. 14). This righteousness is a gift from God, *"their righteousness is from Me" (v. 17),* received through faith and manifested through our obedience to the Divine Direction gained in this month of consecration.

This immunity covers not only physical or material attacks but also verbal assaults: *"every tongue which rises against you in judgment you shall condemn."* Your relentless pursuit of God's face has made you immune to the enemy's schemes. As you step out of this foundational month, do so with the confidence that the unshakeable might of the Almighty God backs the strategic blueprint you hold. Walk in the holiness and the Direction received, and no power on earth or beneath the earth can successfully oppose your God-ordained enlargement, in Jesus' name.

Action: *Reread Isaiah 54:17. Spend five minutes walking around your home or office, loudly and confidently declaring this verse over your family, career, and finances!*

Let us pray

1. *Father, I thank You that my Enlargement is covered by the ultimate promise of immunity, in Jesus' name.*
2. *Holy Spirit, establish me firmly in the righteousness that is gifted by You, in Jesus' name.*
3. *I declare that no weapon formed against me shall prosper, and every negative word spoken is condemned, in Jesus' name.*
4. *Lord, let the Intimacy I have built this month translate into complete security and peace in my life, in Jesus' name.*
5. *I claim my heritage as a servant of the Lord, walking in Divine Direction and complete divine protection, in Jesus' name.*

Saturday 31 January **VALUE COVENANT RELATIONSHIPS**

Read: Ecclesiastes 4:9-12

Bible in 1 year: Deut. 10-12
Bible in 2 years: (Catch-up)

"Though one may be overpowered by another, two can withstand him. And a threefold cord is not quickly broken." (Ecclesiastes 4:12).

The vision of Enlargement in Isaiah 54 is fundamentally a communal mandate; the tent is to be stretched to house a multitude of "Descendants" (v. 3). We are not called to pursue this massive expansion in isolation. Today, we focus on the importance of Covenant relationships—the supportive spiritual community that helps us *stretch* and *strengthen* our stakes. Someone said, "If you want to go fast, go alone. But if you want to go far, go with others." Do you want to go far this year? You must value and maintain healthy relationships.

One of Satan's key strategies is "Separate then strike." I often wonder why God sends some people to us to help liberate and restore them, only for them to disconnect and disappear suddenly. Sadly, when you meet some of them later, they are back in captivity. Stick to those God has brought into your life to help you.

Solomon recognized the spiritual power of unity: *"A threefold cord is not quickly broken" (v. 12)*. The threefold cord is you, your covenant partner, and the Lord Jesus Christ binding you both. The Divine Direction you received in Intimacy is a treasure, but it needs to be guarded and supported by trusted spiritual partners who can lift you when you fall and offer shared wisdom when the path is confusing. Without this support system, the pressures that accompany increased favor and success can quickly lead to isolation and collapse.

Our time of prayer and fasting strengthens the central cord – our intimacy with God. But we must intentionally invest in the horizontal cords of community. This is a practical act of obedience to the Enlargement mandate. Share your vision, seek accountability, and allow others to intercede for your blueprint. Your ability to successfully occupy your enlarged territory is directly linked to the strength of the spiritual alliances you cultivate.

Action: *Identify one covenant friend or spiritual leader who shares your vision for enlargement. Reach out to them today and share one specific challenge you are facing, asking them to stand with you in agreement and intercede for a breakthrough!*

Let us pray
1. *Father, I thank You for the power and protection found in godly covenant relationships, in Jesus' name.*
2. *Holy Spirit, guide me to strong, supportive spiritual partners who will hold the vision for Enlargement with me, in Jesus' name.*
3. *I declare that every spiritual isolation and loneliness assigned against my breakthrough is broken, in Jesus' name.*
4. *Lord, I commit to being a loyal and encouraging covenant partner, helping to stretch the tents of others as well as my own, in Jesus' name.*
5. *Let the strength of the threefold cord guarantee the success and stability of my expanded territory in 2026, in Jesus' name.*

Sunday 1 February   **CROSS INTO THE REALM OF FAITH**

Read: Hebrews 11:1-6

> **Bible in 1 year:** Neh. 1-3
> **Bible in 2 years:** Matt. 3-4

"Now faith is the substance of things hoped for, the evidence of things not seen" (Hebrews 11:1).

Welcome to February! We have successfully completed the foundation of Intimacy and Divine Direction laid in January. Now, we want to cross into the active phase of Enlargement, which is the strategic execution of the blueprint received by faith. Friend, the bridge between the direction or vision you have received from God and its manifestation/ realization is FAITH. Hebrews 11:6 says, *"And without faith it is impossible to please him, for whoever would draw near to God must believe that he exists and that he rewards those who seek him."* In other words, you cannot receive from God without faith.

The instruction to *"Enlarge the place of your tent; stretch out the curtains of your dwellings; do not spare; lengthen your cords..."* in Isaiah 54:2 is an action mandate that demands faith. Faith is the substance, the active step that will transform your hope into tangible reality. Your plan, received in the secret place, is the *"things hoped for"*; now, you must provide the *substance* of Strategic Action to make it real.

True faith is never passive. James says, *"Faith without works [action] is dead" (James 2:17)*. To "Stretch out the curtains" requires effort, courage, and a willingness to step into the unseen. It demands risk.

This month, you must move beyond the spiritual comfort zone of the prayer closet and apply the Divine Direction you have gained. In the Kingdom, we are called to be doers of divine instruction, not just hearers (James 1:22). All the great pioneers of faith in Hebrews 11 acted on the revelation they had received. Noah built an ark to save lives without seeing rain (Hebrews 11:7). Abraham left his country and went to the Promised Land without knowing the clear address (Hebrews 11:8). That is faith! Acting confidently on what God has said even when surrounding circumstances are uncertain.

Your strategic action this month is evidence that you trust God, who has spoken to you, and this will produce great results.

Action: *Write down what you will do by faith this month, pray about it, and start immediately!*

Let us pray
1. *Father, I thank You for the successful foundation laid in January and the clear blueprint for my Enlargement, in Jesus' name.*
2. *Holy Spirit, baptize me with mountain-moving faith to execute the vision and strategically stretch my tent cords, in Jesus' name.*
3. *I declare that this month, my faith will be the substance that manifests the unseen promises into visible reality, in Jesus' name.*
4. *Lord, remove every spiritual and physical obstacle that tries to prevent me from taking the first bold step of my destiny, in Jesus' name.*
5. *I walk out today with courage and conviction, possessing my expanded territory through Strategic Action and faith, in Jesus' name.*

Monday 2 February   **FAITH THAT OPENS THE IMPOSSIBLE**

Read: Matthew 9:18-22

Bible in 1 year: Neh. 4-6
Bible in 2 year: Matt. 5

"Jesus turned, and seeing her he said, 'Take heart, daughter; your faith has made you well.' And instantly the woman was made well" (Matthew 9:22).

Faith that opens impossible doors is active. Faith is more than belief; it is an active trust that moves God's heart and hand. The woman with the issue of blood could have continued in her misery, but instead she believed that touching Jesus' garment would heal her. Jesus told her, *"Daughter, your faith has made you well" (Luke 8:48)*. Her faith was not silent; she acted. She pressed through the crowd, reached out, touched, and instantly received her miracle. Enlargement always follows the moment faith takes action.

Faith that opens doors involves risk. Many believers pray earnestly but stop short of stepping out because fear or doubt holds them back. Peter experienced the supernatural when he stepped out of the boat and walked on water toward Jesus (Matthew 14:29-31). But when he shifted his focus to the storm because of fear, he began to sink. True faith keeps its eyes on Christ – God's promises, not on circumstances. *"For we walk by faith, not by sight" (2 Corinthians 5:7)*. Enlargement – spiritual, financial, or emotional, comes as we dare to move beyond comfort zones and trust God for what seems impossible.

A brother facing overwhelming debt refused to give up but chose to trust God for a breakthrough and provision. Each day, he prayed and courageously visited potential clients. God began to work, and within a few months, his business revived and doubled. This was proof that God honors faith that acts. *"Faith without works is dead" (James 2:26).*

The Greek word *'Pistis'* means "Conviction, firm trust, and total reliance on God's promise that produces corresponding action." Faith is never passive; it works, moves, and opens doors beyond human strength. If you trust God to do it, step out, and you will see His power. Your enlargement will always match the measure of your faith. The more you trust, the more you experience His God's power in your life.

Action: *Identify one area of your life you need to exercise faith and step out!*

Let us pray
1. *Father, thank You for the gift of faith, and Your power to turn impossibilities into testimonies in my life.*
2. *Father, help me to trust Your promises fully, even when the circumstances are discouraging, in Jesus' name.*
3. *O Lord, remove every seed of doubt, fear, or unbelief from my heart, in Jesus' name.*
4. *I receive boldness to act on what I believe God has spoken, in Jesus' name.*
5. *Pray for grace to take the step of faith you have decided on.*

Prophetic Prayers of the Week

1. **"Cleanse your hands… purify your hearts." (James 4:8)** *My hands and my heart will remain pure, in Jesus' name.*
2. *"Let the peace of Christ rule..." (Colossians 3:15). I enjoy uncommon divine peace this year, in Jesus' name.*
3. **"He leads me beside still waters." (Psalm 23:2)** *I receive clear and accurate direction for divine speed this year, in Jesus' name.*

Tuesday 3 February **FAITH THAT OPENS DOORS**

Read: Acts 16:6-10

Bible in 1 year: Neh. 7-9
Bible in 2 years: Matt. 6-7

"...During the night, Paul had a vision of a man of Macedonia standing and begging him, 'Come over to Macedonia and help us'" (Acts 16:9 NIV).

Faith enlarges your capacity to step into new opportunities. The Holy Spirit prevented Paul and his companions from preaching in certain areas. Their response was not resistance or frustration but obedience and trust. Do you still trust God when all the doors are closed against you?

We see in our reading that when Paul obeyed the Spirit, a vision led them to Macedonia – a new territory of blessing in ministry (Acts 16:10). Enlargement often comes when faith aligns with God's direction. So, instead of getting frustrated by the current disappointments and failures, focus on God to show you the door of opportunity He has opened for you.

Friend, faith requires sensitivity to God's guidance. Jesus told His disciples, *"The harvest is plentiful, but the workers are few. Ask the Lord of the harvest to send out workers into His harvest field" (Matthew 9:37-38).* Faith opens doors for ministry when you pray, listen, and step out. It turns closed paths into divine appointments. When God told us to relocate to Yaounde, we didn't have the finances to do the work He had entrusted to us. Doors of provision opened when we stepped out by faith.

Consider Joseph, who had faith in God's promises even as a slave and prisoner (Genesis 39:2-3, 23). His faith opened doors of influence in Potiphar's house and in Egypt. Similarly, Esther's faith opened the door to save a nation (Esther 4:14-16). Faith always positions you where God can multiply your life. Trust God and be willing to step out and do His will.

"Faith" is Greek *'Pistis'*, which carries the sense of "Trust, reliance, and confident expectation." Faith activates divine direction and supernatural openings. Without faith, doors remain closed; with faith, God leads you into enlargement.

Friend, your next level of blessing is waiting behind a door only faith can unlock. Step through in faith today!

Action: *Identify one area where God is prompting you and take the first obedient step in faith.*

Let us pray

1. *Thank You, Lord, for opening doors of opportunity in my life through faith, in Jesus' name.*
2. *Lord, give me sensitivity to Your Spirit's guidance, in Jesus' name.*
3. *Father, deliver my soul from hesitation and fear that prevent me from stepping into new opportunities, in Jesus' name.*
4. *Father, help me to trust Your timing and follow Your leading without delay, in Jesus' name.*
5. *Lord, enlarge my capacity to walk into God-ordained opportunities and assignments, in Jesus' name.*

Wednesday 4 February   **ASK GOD FOR A STRATEGY**

Read: 1 Samuel 16:1-5

Bible in 1 year: Neh. 10-13
Bible in 2 years: Matt. 8-9

"If any of you lacks wisdom, you should ask God, who gives generously to all without finding fault, and it will be given to you" (James 1:5).

Every divine assignment requires a divine strategy. Samuel was sent to anoint David as king, but the mission carried great risk. If Saul discovered it, Samuel's life would be in danger. A lesser prophet might have rushed forward recklessly or shrank back in fear, but Samuel did the right thing; he asked God how to proceed. God gave him a wise strategy: go under the cover of a sacrifice. This way, the mission was accomplished without exposing Samuel to premature death.

This biblical account shows us that the Holy Spirit not only gives revelation (word of knowledge) but also instruction (word of wisdom). Revelation tells us *what* is to come; wisdom shows us *how* to act. Many believers receive vision but fail because they lack a strategy. Jesus said the Spirit will *"Teach you all things" (John 14:26)* and *"show you things to come" (John 16:13)*. The role of the Holy Spirit is not only to REVEAL but to GUIDE.

Consider Joshua at Jericho. God did not simply promise victory; He gave a strategy – march around the city for seven days, then shout (Joshua 6:2-5). Victory followed because the strategy was obeyed. Likewise, Jesus taught Peter to cast his net on the RIGHT side of the boat for a miraculous catch (John 21:6). That was precision!

A sister in business experienced a breakthrough during a financial crisis, when she prayed and received divine wisdom. God gave her a specific strategy to restructure her work. Following it, she not only overcame the situation but also expanded.

Are you facing risk, opposition, or a challenging assignment? Don't rely solely on human wisdom. Ask God for His strategy. Divine strategy secures divine results.

Action: *Fast for at least one day this week and ask God for a strategy to change that situation!*

Let us pray
1. *Father, thank You for being the God who gives wise strategies for every assignment, in Jesus' name.*
2. *Lord, give me ears to hear Your instructions and the humility to follow them, in Jesus' name.*
3. *Father, grant me the wisdom to handle risky situations without fear, in Jesus' name.*
4. *Dear Holy Spirit, help me align the word of knowledge with the word of wisdom in my life, in Jesus' name.*
5. *Let every plan of the enemy against my mission be frustrated by divine strategy, in Jesus' name.*
6. *I declare: I will not fail because God's wisdom is my strategy for victory, in Jesus' name.*

Thursday 5 February   **WHAT IS DRIVING YOU?**

Read: Hebrews 10:32-39

> **Bible in 1 year:** Est. 1-4
> **Bible in 2 years:** Matt. 10

"Now the just shall live by faith; but if anyone draws back, My soul has no pleasure in him." (Hebrews 10:38).

Every person is driven by something, and what drives you will ultimately determine your destination. It's not just where you are today that matters, but what is pushing you forward. The force that drives you determines the outcome of your life – your joy, your peace, your success, and even your failures.

Two powerful forces drive people in life: FAITH and FEAR. Fear is rooted in uncertainty. It whispers, "The future is uncertain. It won't work out for you." Fear is the belief that things won't turn out the way you hope, and it often paralyzes you with worry. It causes you to doubt your abilities, your worth, and God's promises. Fear leads to inaction, to standing still, and to shrinking back. It flows from ignorance, from believing lies, and from putting trust in your own ability rather than in God's power.

On the other hand, FAITH is a powerful force that believes the future is secure because of God's faithfulness. Faith says, "Even if I don't see the whole picture, I know that my future is guaranteed because God is with me." Faith declares, "I will succeed, not because of my own strength, but because Jesus Christ is walking with me." Faith says, "It shall be well with me, because the Creator of the universe is by my side."

Faith is generated by revelation – by seeing things as God sees them. Faith is grounded in understanding His Word and being fully convinced of His promises. It takes action, steps of obedience, and a heart set on trusting God, even when we don't know exactly where He's leading us.

Abraham understood this force of faith. In Hebrews 11:8, it says, *"By faith Abraham obeyed when he was called to go out to the place which he would receive as an inheritance. And he went out, not knowing where he was going."* Abraham trusted God's plan for him, even when the future seemed uncertain. His faith was the force that drove him to obedience.

Action: *Identify one negative thought that is resisting your faith. Begin to uproot it with God's Word.*

Let us pray
1. *Father, thank You because Your Word cannot fail in my life, in Jesus' name.*
2. *Father, strengthen me in the spirit to focus on what You're doing in my life, and not on what Satan is doing, in Jesus' name.*
3. *Fire of God, burn in my soul and wipe out every voice that contradicts God's voice, in Jesus' name.*
4. *Father, You have planned a glorious future for me in Christ; I will not end on the way, in Jesus' name.*
5. *Father, several believers are facing persecution globally; strengthen their love and faith in Christ.*

Friday 6 February

THE GOD WHO DEFENDS YOUR PORTION

Read: Proverbs 23:10-11

Bible in 1 year: Est. 5-7
Bible in 2 years: Matt. 11; 12:1-23

"For their Redeemer is strong; He will take up their case against you" (Proverbs 23:11).

There are moments in life when it feels as if something is trying to push you out of the place God gave you. Sometimes it's people. Sometimes it's circumstances. Sometimes it's fear whispering that you will lose what God promised.

In ancient Israel, boundary stones marked the inheritance God assigned to each family. To move a boundary stone was to steal destiny, identity, and provision. But God in today's reading declared a powerful truth: He Himself defends the boundary lines of His people.

Our key verse says, *"Their Redeemer is strong."* The One who bought your life by the blood of Jesus is not passive. This year, He will step into battles you cannot fight. He will argue any case you cannot handle. He will guard the territory you cannot protect by your own strength.

Perhaps, today you feel like something is trying to shift your boundary – your peace, your calling, your opportunities, your family, your progress. Maybe you sense resistance, sabotage, or intimidation from somewhere or someone. The Scripture reminds you: IF GOD GAVE YOU A PORTION, NO ONE CAN TAKE IT. God does not just give; He guards. He does not just promise; He protects.

When you have no words, He becomes your Advocate. When you have no strength, He becomes your Defender. When you have no clarity, He becomes your Judge who rules in your favor. Your inheritance is not fragile. It is not at the mercy of people. It is not vulnerable to manipulation. It is held in the hands of your strong Redeemer.

Today, stand tall in this truth: What God has assigned to you cannot be taken, moved, or stolen. Your Redeemer is strong – and He fights for you.

Action: *Speak aloud today what God has given you – your peace, your calling, your family, your purpose – and declare that your boundaries are secure in Christ.*

Let us pray
1. *Lord, I thank You for being my strong Redeemer and faithful Defender, in Jesus' name.*
2. *Father, guard every area of my life where I feel pressured or threatened, in Jesus' name.*
3. *Lord, restore any portion of my inheritance that has been stolen or weakened, in Jesus' name.*
4. *Redeemer of my soul, take up my case and fight every battle beyond my strength, in Jesus' name.*
5. *I decree that my God-given boundaries, blessings, and destiny shall not be moved, stolen, or altered, in Jesus' name.*

Saturday 7 February   **RUN TO THE CITY OF REFUGE**

Read: Numbers 35:9-15

Bible in 1 year: Est. 8-10
Bible in 2 years: Matt. 12:24-50; 13:1-23

"The name of the LORD is a strong tower; the righteous run to it and are safe" (Proverbs 18:10).

In the Old Testament, God commanded Israel to establish cities of refuge – safe havens/locations for those who had accidentally committed manslaughter. These cities were not for the guilty in intent, but for those who needed protection from revenge while justice was served. The principle is clear: when danger, accusation, or pressure comes, God provides a safe place where His justice and mercy meet.

Spiritually, the city of refuge represents Christ. When life's trials, attacks, or false accusations come your way, you are called to run to Jesus, the ultimate sanctuary. Just as the Israelites fled to these cities to be safe from the avenger of blood, you can flee to God in prayer, obedience, and faith for protection, guidance, and deliverance.

Today's story teaches several lessons:

1. ***Recognize Danger Early*** – Just as the Israelites had to flee immediately, you must identify spiritual, emotional, or relational dangers before they destroy you.
2. ***Act Quickly*** – Delay can be fatal. Running to God immediately prevents panic, despair, or spiritual defeat.
3. ***Stay Within the Refuge*** – Once you reach God's protection, remain in His Word, His presence, and His

peace until the threat is over. Do not return prematurely to danger or compromise.

4. ***Trust God's Justice*** – The city of refuge protected the innocent while the guilty faced judgment. Trust that God's timing and judgment are perfect. He will defend the innocent and deal with the wicked in His time.

Action: *Are you facing attacks, accusations, or overwhelming pressure? Run to Jesus now!*

Let us pray
1. *Lord, I thank You for being my city of refuge and hiding place in every trial.*
2. *Father, help me to recognize danger early and flee to Your protection immediately.*
3. *O Lord, help me to remain in Your presence until You deliver me completely.*
4. *Father, protect me from the plans of the enemy and turn every attack into testimony.*
5. *I decree that no accusation, attack, or scheme of the enemy will touch me, for I dwell in the refuge of the Almighty.*

Sunday 8 February **JESUS CHRIST YOUR HUSBAND**

Read: Isaiah 54:4-11

Bible in 1 year: Dan. 1-3
Bible in 2 years: Matt. 13:24-58; 14

"For your Maker is your husband—the LORD of hosts is His name; and your Redeemer is the Holy One of Israel; He is called the God of the whole earth" (Isaiah 54:5).

When Isaiah calls God your "Husband," he uses language meant to settle your heart in seasons when you feel forgotten or overwhelmed. A husband in ancient Israel wasn't just a romantic partner – he was protector, provider, defender, and covenant keeper. To say *"your Maker is your Husband"* means the One who designed every detail of your life is also the One who binds Himself to you with unbreakable commitment.

Isaiah 54:5-10 paints a picture of a God who may allow moments that feel like distance, but only to gather you in with greater compassion. His brief anger is swallowed up in everlasting kindness. His covenant of peace stands firmer than ancient mountains.

A woman once shared how she walked through a painful season of betrayal from her husband and loneliness. She clung to this very passage, whispering daily, "Lord, if You are truly my Husband, then hold me where others let go." Day by day, she experienced unexpected provision, comfort, and strength. Later, she testified, "When everyone else disappeared, Jesus showed me He wasn't symbolic; He was real. He carried me like a faithful Husband." This story mirrors the heart of Isaiah 54: God doesn't love you vaguely; He loves you personally and covenantally.

"Maker" is Hebrew *'Asah'*, which means "One who skillfully fashions. "Husband" is Hebrew *'Ba'al'*, meaning "Master, protector, covenant partner." "Redeemer" is Hebrew *Go'el'*, meaning "The family defender who rescues at personal cost." These are not poetic labels; they clearly describe the profound relationship we have with God. Beloved, Jesus Christ is all of these toward you. You are not forsaken. You are not alone. You are held by covenant love.

Action: *Speak to Jesus today as your Husband. Tell Him where you need His comfort, His strength, and His covenant faithfulness!*

Let us pray

1. *Lord, thank You for being my faithful Husband and Redeemer, in Jesus' name.*
2. *O Lord, heal every place in my heart where I have felt abandoned or forgotten, in Jesus' name.*
3. *Father, let Your everlasting kindness steady me in every shaking, in Jesus' name.*
4. *Lord, reveal Yourself to me as Protector, Provider, and Covenant Keeper daily, in Jesus' name.*
5. *I decree that Your covenant of peace will stand unshaken in my life forever, in Jesus' name.*

Monday 9 February   **GOD'S WISDOM FOR BUSINESS GROWTH**

Read: Proverbs 24:3-7

Bible in 1 year: Dan. 4-6
Bible in 2 years: Matt. 15-16

"By wisdom a house is built" (Proverbs 24:3).

Every business, whether big or small, needs more than capital. It requires wisdom, understanding, and knowledge. Many people in our communities start small businesses out of necessity, but they do not take the time to seek God's wisdom or to learn simple principles that guarantee success.

The Bible teaches that wisdom is the foundation of any stable structure (Proverbs 4:7). A business built on guesswork will always struggle, but one built on God's wisdom and sound financial principles will endure challenges and grow. According to a USA study, "About 21.5% of private-sector businesses fail within their first year. Roughly 48–50% of businesses will close within five years. Beyond ten years, about 65% of businesses have closed; only 35% survive to year ten."

Wisdom helps you choose the right location, understand your customers, price your goods correctly, and manage your finances effectively. Understanding enables you to discern why your sales rise or fall. Knowledge helps you improve your product and better serve people.

God is not opposed to business; He delights in the progress of His people (Psalm 35:27). Jesus Himself taught more parables about stewardship, money, and diligence than on almost any other topic. He wants your hands to be productive. But He also expects you to work with discipline, honesty, and excellence.

When you combine prayer with practical action, God blesses the work of your hands. He multiplies the little you have and opens doors that others cannot shut. So, ask Him daily for wisdom to make decisions. Ask Him for understanding to know your customers. Ask Him for knowledge to improve your work. As you apply godly principles, you will see your small business turn into a stable source of blessing.

Action: *Ask God for wisdom today and write down one practical step you will take to improve your business!*

Let us pray
1. *Lord, give me wisdom to manage my business well.*
2. *Father, guide me in making the right decisions daily.*
3. *Lord, teach me how to serve my customers with excellence.*
4. *Father, bless the work of my hands and expand my opportunities.*
5. *O Lord, protect my business from loss, bad decisions, and discouragement.*

Prophetic Prayers of the Week
1. **"Keep yourself pure." (1 Timothy 5:22)** *Nothing will defile my spiritual garment, in Jesus' name.*
2. **"You will break out on the right and on the left." (Isaiah 54:3)** *My enlargement this month is unstoppable, in Jesus' name.*
3. **"Write the vision…" (Habakkuk 2:2)** *Nothing will steal my God-given vision this year, in Jesus' name.*

Tuesday 10 February   **BE THE CHANGE YOU WANT TO SEE**

Read: Matthew 5:13-16;
Philippians 2:14-16

Bible in 1 year: Dan. 7-9
Bible in 2 years: Matt. 17-18

"In everything set them an example by doing what is good" (Titus 2:7 NIV).

Everyone, even believers, dream of a better nation – one marked by justice, peace, honesty, and love. But change does not begin with government, systems, or policies alone; it starts with individuals. You can make a difference in this nation by becoming the very person you wish others would be where you live or serve.

In Matthew 5:13-16, Jesus calls us the salt of the earth and the light of the world. Salt preserves; light exposes and guides. These qualities are not just spoken but lived out in daily actions. The Greek word for "example" in Titus 2:7, *'Typos'*, means "a pattern to be imitated." Before we can inspire transformation in others, we must first embody it ourselves.

If you wish your nation had more honesty, start by refusing to cheat in small matters. If you desire unity, be the one who refuses to spread gossip or division. Just as a single candle can light many others, your personal integrity and godliness can ignite change in those around you.

Philippians 2:14-16 urges us to *"shine like stars"* in a crooked generation. Stars do not compete with darkness; they shine, and the darkness cannot extinguish them.

Likewise, you may not be able to change everyone, but you can live in such a way that your life becomes a living invitation for others to follow.

Lasting national change is the fruit of personal transformation multiplied across a people. If every believer decided to live the Christ-like life they wish to see in others, revival would sweep across nations.

As you go out today, *"Let your light so shine before men that they may see your good works and glorify your Father who is in heaven" (Matthew 5:16).*

Action: *Do one thing in your house or workplace today that will manifest Christ's love to somebody!*

Let us pray
1. *Father, thank You for calling me to be salt and light in this generation, in Jesus' name.*
2. *Father, transform my character to reflect Christ in all I do, in Jesus' name.*
3. *Father, help me model the virtues I want to see in my nation, in Jesus' name.*
4. *Father, let my life inspire others toward righteousness and nation building, in Jesus' name.*
5. *Father, pour Your Spirit in the Church and make every Christian in this nation an agent of change, in Jesus' name.*

Wednesday 11 February **A BLESSED CITIZEN**

Read: Ephesians 2:19-22

Bible in 1 year: Dan. 10-12
Bible in 2 years: Matt. 19-20

"Now, therefore, you are no longer strangers and foreigners, but fellow citizens with the saints and members of the household of God" (Ephesians 2:19).

Do you know that citizenship is an extraordinary privilege? My brothers, who are American citizens, enjoy the freedom to travel across more than 150 nations without visa stress, while I often have to stand in long embassy lines, fill out endless forms, and wait for approval. Their nationality grants them access to rights, protection, and opportunities that I cannot enjoy without the same citizenship. It offers them a sense of belonging and confidence wherever they go.

In a far greater and more glorious way, the apostle Paul reminds believers that we have become *citizens of heaven* through Christ Jesus. This divine citizenship is far superior to any earthly nationality. It gives us access to the presence of God, the forgiveness of sins, and the full privileges of being sons and daughters of His Kingdom. Once strangers and foreigners to the promises of God, we are now members of His household – loved, accepted, and empowered to represent Him on earth. Wherever we go, we carry the authority and identity of heaven.

A missionary once serving in a war-torn region was asked if he feared for his life. He smiled and said, "My true citizenship is in heaven; that passport guarantees my eternal safety." What a powerful perspective! Friend, this understanding will free you from fear and anchor your loyalty and confidence in God's Kingdom rather than in earthly systems.

However, every citizenship comes with responsibilities. As citizens of heaven, we are called to live as ambassadors (2 Corinthians 5:18-20), faithfully representing our King through holiness, humility, love, and unity. Our lives should reflect the character of our homeland, heaven.

Charles Spurgeon once said, *"If heaven is your home, live as though you're headed there."* Let this truth guide your words, thoughts, and actions as you step out today. Remember, you are not an ordinary person; you are heaven's representative on earth.

Declaration: *I am a citizen of heaven, and I will reflect God's Kingdom wherever I go.*

Let us pray
1. *Father, thank You for making me a citizen of Your heavenly Kingdom, in Jesus' name.*
2. *Lord, empower me to faithfully represent You in all I do, in Jesus' name.*
3. *Father, help me walk daily in the blessings and authority of my heavenly citizenship, in Jesus' name.*
4. *Father, teach me to seek Your Kingdom above earthly ambitions, in Jesus' name.*
5. *Father, unite Your children to effectively expand Your Kingdom on earth, in Jesus' name.*
6. *Father, grant me courage to proclaim boldly my heavenly identity wherever I go, in Jesus' name.*

Thursday 12 February   **STAND YOUR GROUND**

Read: Nehemiah 6:10-14

Bible in 1 year: 1 Thess. 1-3
Bible in 2 years: Matt. 21

"But I replied, 'Should someone in my position run from danger? Should someone in my position enter the Temple to save his life? No, I won't do it!'" (Nehemiah 6:11 NLT).

Whenever you begin to do a good work for God – whether in ministry, family, or community, the enemy will rise with schemes to stop you. Nehemiah faced constant opposition as he rebuilt Jerusalem's walls. His enemies tried intimidation, manipulation, false prophecy, and threats, but he refused to be moved. He declared, *"Should someone in my position run from danger? No, I won't do it!" (v.11)*. He stood his ground.

"Stand" in Hebrew is *'Amad'*, meaning "To remain, to endure, to hold one's position." To stand your ground is to remain unshaken in the face of opposition.

The devil's goal is always the same: to sap your courage and discredit your calling. He may send messengers of bad news to drain your joy, spread messages of fear to paralyze your progress, or raise false prophets to manipulate your decisions. As Nehemiah said in verse 13, *"They were hoping to intimidate me and make me sin. Then they would be able to accuse and discredit me."* But because Nehemiah stood firm, their plots failed, and the work was completed.

In Christ, we are called to stand our ground. Paul exhorts us: *"Put on the full armor of God, so that when the day of evil comes, you may be able to stand your ground" (Ephesians 6:13).* Standing does not mean passivity; it means refusing to yield to fear, compromise, or distraction. Like Jesus, who stood His ground in Gethsemane and triumphed at the cross, God will strengthen you to finish the work He has given you.

In church, false accusations rose against a pastor during a building project. Instead of quitting, he kept praying and working. In the end, the project was completed, and even his accusers acknowledged God's hand.

Friend, no matter the threats or manipulations, God is calling you to stand your ground. Victory belongs to those who refuse to run.

Action: *Write down your commitment to stand your ground concerning what you are facing now.*

Let us pray

1. *Father, thank You for giving me courage and strength to stand firm, in Jesus' name.*
2. *Father, deliver me from fear, intimidation, and manipulation, in Jesus' name.*
3. *Father, guard me against false voices and negative prophecies that seek to derail me, in Jesus' name.*
4. *O Lord, strengthen me to remain focused on the work You have given me, in Jesus' name.*
5. *Father, arise, let every plan to discredit or discourage me be frustrated, in Jesus' name.*
6. *I declare: I will stand my ground, finish my assignment, and overcome every opposition, in Jesus' name.*

Friday 13 February   **PRIORITIZE THE ESSENTIALS**

Read: Matthew 6:25-34

Bible in 1 year: Josh. 1-3
Bible in 2 years: Matt. 22

"But seek first the kingdom of God and His righteousness, and all these things shall be added to you." (Matthew 6:33).

The success of Strategic Action lies not just in diligence, but in Prioritization – the wisdom to focus your energy on the actions that yield the most remarkable results. In today's reading, Jesus establishes the strategic cornerstone of life: seeking the Kingdom first. This principle must be applied directly to your Enlargement blueprint.

When executing the mandate to *stretch out* and *lengthen your cords* (Isaiah 54:2), you cannot afford to treat all tasks equally. If you try to do everything at once, you will become scattered, weary, and lose momentum. Strategic Action requires identifying the single most crucial action item with the highest strategic impact – the 20% of effort that will produce 80% of your breakthrough, and executing it first.

The Divine Direction received in January is your strategic guide, pointing you to the actions that align with the Kingdom's purpose for your life. By prioritizing these high-impact tasks, you are essentially seeking God's righteousness (His way of doing things) for your expansion. This focused effort ensures efficiency, prevents burnout, and guarantees that "all these things" (the visible manifestation of the enlarged territory) shall be added to you.

Action: *Before you begin your day, review your to-do list. Prayerfully identify the single highest-priority action (the strategic cornerstone) required to move your enlargement blueprint forward. Commit to executing this one task with diligence and discipline before you move on to anything else.*

Let us pray

1. *Father, I thank You for the wisdom of the Kingdom that directs my priorities, in Jesus' name.*
2. *Holy Spirit, release the spirit of discernment, helping me to identify the highest-impact actions in my blueprint, in Jesus' name.*
3. *I declare that I will seek first Your will for my Enlargement, and all necessary resources will be added to me, in Jesus' name.*
4. *Lord, remove every distraction and grant me laser-like focus to execute my Strategic Action with maximum efficiency, in Jesus' name.*
5. *I will walk in wisdom and disciplined prioritization, ensuring that my greatest efforts yield my greatest results, in Jesus' name.*

Saturday 14 February — **MAKE YOUR MARRIAGE HONORABLE**

Read: Hebrews 13:4-6

Bible in 1 year: Josh. 4-6
Bible in 2 years: Matt. 23

"Marriage is honorable among all, and the bed undefiled; but fornicators and adulterers God will judge" (Hebrews 13:4).

Marriage is God's gift, created to be honorable, sweet, fruitful, and blessed. When God made Adam and Eve, He said, *"It is not good for the man to be alone,"* and blessed their union. Yet, not every marriage reflects God's honor. Some marriages are full of shame, pain, frustration, and discord.

Hebrews 13:4 reveals the two pillars of an honorable marriage: HONOR THE COVENANT and KEEP THE MARRIAGE BED UNDEFILED. Before we explore these, we must recognize what makes a marriage dishonorable: sexual unfaithfulness, abuse, lack of communication, irresponsibility, disrespect, and outside interference.

Like a brand-new car left unserviced, marriages neglected spiritually and practically break down. God calls us to nurture our marriages intentionally.

5 Rules for making your marriage honorable:
1. *Honor Each Other:* Speak kindly, appreciate strengths, and never shame your spouse publicly.

2. **Keep the Marriage Bed Undefiled:** Maintain sexual purity, avoid adultery and pornography, and protect intimacy intentionally. "Pure" is the Greek *'Hagnos'*, meaning "Morally upright, and undefiled." In marriage, it implies not only physical faithfulness but also emotional and spiritual loyalty. A pure marriage honors God and protects your union from corruption.
3. **Practice Open Communication:** Share daily your fears, plans, finances, and spiritual life.
4. **Walk in Love and Forgiveness:** No spouse is perfect. Forgive quickly and reject bitterness.
5. **Involve God:** Pray together, study the Word, and invite His presence into your home.

Action: *What must you stop or start doing for your marriage to succeed? Begin to do it now!*

Let us pray
1. *Father, thank You for the gift of a spouse, in Jesus' name.*
2. *Lord, help me make my marriage honorable and full of Your blessings, in Jesus' name.*
3. *I break every spirit of unfaithfulness and impurity attacking my marriage, in Jesus' name.*
4. *I destroy every generational curse or pattern causing harm in my home, in Jesus' name.*
5. *Merciful Father, release love, wisdom, and understanding between me and my spouse.*
6. *Pray for the unmarried in your family to experience the restoration of their marital destinies.*

Sunday 15 February **WHAT IS EATING YOU UP?**

Read: Psalm 32:1-5

> Bible in 1 year: Josh. 7-9
> Bible in 2 years: Matt. 24

"He who covers his sins will not prosper, but whoever confesses and forsakes them will have mercy" (Proverbs 28:13).

Are you struggling to cover up a sin you have committed? God wants you to confess it and obtain forgiveness and freedom.

"*Confess*" in Hebrew is '*Yadah*', meaning to "Acknowledge, admit openly, or cast down." True confession is not just admission but the release of the burden by exposing it before God.

Secrets have a way of eating one from the inside out. Hidden sin, unresolved trauma, or unspoken struggles act like termites, silently destroying foundations.

David learned this truth. He hid his sin with Bathsheba until Nathan confronted him. His confession in Psalm 32 reveals the cost of secrecy: *"When I kept silent, my bones wasted away through my groaning all day long"* (v.3). Silence drained his strength, but confession brought restoration.

What is eating you up may not only be guilt but also relational and spiritual poverty. Many live surrounded by hundreds of online connections, yet lack one friend who will tell them the truth. Solomon, David's son, reminds us: *"Wounds from a sincere friend are better than many kisses from an enemy" (Proverbs 27:6)*. True freedom often requires exposing secrets to God and trusted friends who walk in truth.

David's story warns us that unchecked secrecy grows into destruction. But Christ bore your sins openly on the cross (1 Peter 2:24). He is inviting you to confess your sins, not to shame you, but to heal you. James 5:16 confirms this: *"Confess your sins to each other and pray for each other so that you may be healed."* Healing flows when we bring darkness into the light of Christ.

A man once confessed his addiction to a trusted prayer partner. For years, shame isolated him, but the moment he opened up, he found accountability, freedom, and renewal. His secret lost its power the day he exposed it to God's light.

What is eating you up? Don't cover it, confess it. Expose it. Christ's mercy is greater than your secret.

Action: *Confess that secret that has been eating you up to someone today!*

Let us pray

1. *Father, thank You for the mercy and freedom available through Christ, in Jesus' name.*
2. *Lord, search my heart and expose anything hidden that hinders my walk with You, in Jesus' name.*
3. *Father, grant me courage to confess and release every secret burden, in Jesus' name.*
4. *Father, surround me with godly friends who sharpen, challenge, and correct me, in Jesus' name.*
5. *Father, deliver me from the bondage of secrecy and isolation; let healing flow into every area of my life, in Jesus' name.*

Monday 16 February   **PEACE IN THE STORM**

Read: Mark 4:35-41;
Philippians 4:6-7

Bible in 1 year: Josh. 10-12
Bible in 2 years: Matt. 25

"He got up, rebuked the wind and said to the waves, 'Peace! Be still!' Then the wind died down and it was completely calm" (Mark 4:39 NIV).

Storms are part of life. They come in the form of sickness, financial crises, broken relationships, or spiritual battles. The disciples experienced a storm of life when waves threatened to sink their boat. Panic filled their hearts, but Jesus was asleep, unshaken by the chaos. When they cried out, He rose and spoke, *"Peace! Be still!"* and the storm instantly ceased.

The Greek word for peace here is *'Eirēnē,'* meaning tranquility that results from divine order. Jesus did not merely quiet the storm; He re-established heaven's order in creation. His authority proved that storms do not define destiny; His Word does.

Philippians 4:6-7 adds another dimension: *"Do not be anxious about anything, but in every situation, by prayer and petition, with thanksgiving, present your requests to God. And the peace of God, which transcends all understanding, will guard your hearts and your minds in Christ Jesus."* This peace is a garrison, protecting us from fear while storms rage.

Corrie Ten Boom survived Nazi concentration camps. She said, "There is no pit so deep that God's love is not deeper still." Even in prison, she radiated peace because Christ's presence guarded her heart. Like the disciples, she discovered that the storm may roar outside, but Jesus calms the storm within.

You may not control the storm, but you can choose to invite Jesus into your boat. His peace is not circumstantial; it is supernatural. Storms in your life test your faith, but they also reveal Jesus' power. When Christ is with you, storms become testimonies of His authority.

That storm you are facing now will not destroy you; it will reposition you for your next level, in Jesus' name.

Action: *Are you facing a storm? Ask your spiritual authority to pray peace over you!*

Let us pray
1. *Father, step into every storm of my life and speak peace, in Jesus' name.*
2. *Father, guard my heart and mind with Your peace that surpasses human understanding, in Jesus' name.*
3. *Holy Spirit, teach me to trust God even when storms rage, in Jesus' name.*
4. *Lord, let every storm around my family and nation be stilled now, in Jesus' name.*
5. *Prince of Peace, make me an agent of calmness in turbulent times, in Jesus' name.*

Prophetic Prayers of the Week
1. **"The Lord has given you the city." (Joshua 6:2)** *I possess my possessions in this city this week, in Jesus' name.*

2. ***"They came to life and stood up." (Ezekiel 37:10).*** *I speak life to every dry place in my life and destiny, in Jesus' name.*
3. ***"Your ears shall hear a word behind you…" (Isaiah 30:21)*** *I receive divine direction as I step out today, in Jesus' name.*

Tuesday 17 February **KEEP YOUR CONSCIENCE PURE**

Read: 2 Corinthians 6:1-10

Bible in 1 year: Josh. 13-15
Bible in 2 years: Matt. 26

We don't want anyone to find fault with our work, and so we try hard not to cause problems" (2 Corinthians 6:3 CEV).

A pure conscience is one of the greatest treasures you can possess as a believer. God looks beyond our activities and examines the motives that drive them. In a generation that celebrates achievement, speed, and results, we are reminded that what truly matters to God is the condition of our hearts.

You can perform impressive deeds and still miss God's approval if the motives behind them are corrupted. Heaven values purity far more than outward success. Paul understood this deeply. He desired not only to avoid sin but also to live in such a way that nothing, whether intentional or unintentional, would discredit the name of Christ. His life and ministry flowed from an inner purity that governed his actions, relationships, and decisions.

In his writings, Paul repeatedly emphasizes the importance of a clear conscience. He said, *"I strive always to keep my conscience clear before God and man" (Acts 24:16)*. He acknowledged that even though his conscience was clear, the final judgment belonged to God (1 Corinthians 4:4). He taught that genuine love springs from *"a pure heart, a good conscience, and sincere faith" (1 Timothy 1:5)*. He urged believers to hold tightly to faith and a good conscience (1 Timothy 1:19). He testified that he served God *"with a clear conscience" (2 Timothy 1:3).*

The Scriptures also warn against silencing the voice of your conscience through repeated compromise (1 Timothy 4:2) and call us to escape the moral corruption of the world through God's divine power (2 Peter 1:3-4). In everyday life, pressures can push us toward shortcuts, pretense, exaggeration, and dishonesty. But God invites us, His children, to walk the narrow path of sincerity and holiness.

A clear conscience brings peace, freedom, and confidence before God. A troubled conscience drains strength and steals joy. As believers, we must allow the Holy Spirit to search our hearts and correct us. God's grace is not a license to live carelessly; it is the power to live purely. May we, like Paul, serve with a conscience that honors God and reflects Christ to the world.

Action: *Examine your heart today. If anything is troubling your conscience, confess it, make it right, and ask the Holy Spirit to restore your inner purity!*

Let us pray

1. *Lord, give me a sensitive and obedient conscience that responds quickly to Your voice, in Jesus' name.*
2. *Father, purify my motives and cleanse my heart from hidden faults, in Jesus' name.*
3. *Holy Spirit, deliver me from every form of compromise and dishonesty, in Jesus' name.*
4. *Lord, help me to live with integrity so that my life does not discredit the gospel, in Jesus' name.*

5. *Father, strengthen me with grace to walk daily in sincerity, purity, and truth, in Jesus' name.*

Wednesday 18 February **HOW NOT TO FADE AWAY**

Read: Revelation 2:1-7

Bible in 1 year: Josh. 16-18
Bible in 2 years: Matt. 27

"Nevertheless, I have this against you: You have forsaken the love you had at first. Remember the height from which you have fallen. Repent and do the things you did at first" (Revelation 2:4-5).

Starting well does not guarantee finishing well. Many leaders, ministries, and Christian organizations begin with zeal, clarity, and divine purpose but gradually drift, compromise, or lose focus.

Spiritually, "Fading away" is the slow loss of vitality, passion, and sensitivity to God. A person may appear busy, active, or even successful, yet inwardly be dry, guilty, or disconnected. Activity without life, service without intimacy, and duties without devotion are hallmarks of fading. A spiritually fading believer is like a lamp whose wick burns dimly – still lit, but not giving enough light to guide others or illuminate their own path.

The Greek word *'Aphanizo'* means "To disappear, vanish, or become invisible gradually." Spiritually, it represents the subtle, almost imperceptible process by which a believer loses influence, passion, and clarity of purpose. Fading does not happen overnight; it creeps in through neglect, compromise, and distraction. It contrasts with *'Nupho'*, which means "To be alert, vigilant, and spiritually sober." The Spirit calls us to remain awake and vigilant to avoid this silent spiritual decline.

Imagine a once-vibrant fire slowly covered with ash and dust. From a distance, it may look like it is still burning, but the heat and light are fading. Only when the ash is removed and the embers are stirred does the fire regain its strength. Likewise, a believer must remove distractions, repent from sin, and return to intimacy with God to reignite spiritual life and passion. This is the message Jesus sent to the Church in Ephesus, and He is reechoing it to us today.

To maintain spiritual clarity, integrity, and focus, you must return to your first love, practice daily obedience, seek accountability, and prioritize intimacy with God above activity. Fading is preventable, but it requires vigilance, humility, and renewed devotion.

Action: *Pray and reflect on areas where you may be drifting; recommit today to your first love and purpose in God!*

Let us pray
1. *Father, thank You for calling me into a vibrant relationship with You, in Jesus' name.*
2. *Lord, reveal every area where I am fading spiritually, in Jesus' name.*
3. *Father, restore the passion and devotion I had at first for you, in Jesus' name.*
4. *Lord, give me clarity, integrity, and focus to finish strong, in Jesus' name.*
5. *I decree that I will not fade away but remain fruitful, radiant, and spiritually alive, in Jesus' name.*

Thursday 19 February　　　**GOD TAKES TIME TO DO CERTAIN THINGS**

Read: *Acts 13:17-20*

Bible in 1 year: Josh. 19-21
Bible in 2 years: Matt. 28; Ex. 1

"And I am sure of this, that he who began a good work in you will bring it to completion at the day of Jesus Christ" (Philippians 1:6).

We live in an impatient world. People are losing the ability to wait for anything. From instant messaging to fast food to next-day delivery, we have been conditioned to expect speed, even with God. But God is not in a hurry. He does not operate on man's stopwatch.

Interestingly, Acts 13:20 reminds us that God took 450 years to fulfill the promise He made to Abraham – delivering Israel, training them, and settling them in their inheritance. Why? Because God does things perfectly and completely, and not in a hurry.

He is not only the Alpha but the Omega. He does not begin what He will not finish. Philippians 1:6 assures us, *"He who began a good work in you will carry it on to completion."* The Greek word for "Completion" is '*Epiteleō*,' meaning to bring to perfect fulfillment. Dear friend, God is not experimenting with your life. He is executing a divine blueprint. He has a plan, a process, and a perfect timeline concerning you.

There are divine principles that govern how He works. He plans before He acts. He operates in justice, never violating righteousness. He trains before He uses. He multiplies before He sends. And He never uses shortcuts. Even Jesus, God in the flesh, had to grow in wisdom and stature before beginning His ministry at 30 (Luke 2:40, 51-52).

Imagine a builder constructing a skyscraper. The deeper the foundation, the longer the delay before anything visible rises. But when the building finally appears, it is unshakable. God works like that. What seems like a delay is often divine preparation. Some promises may take longer than expected, not because God has forgotten, but because He is ensuring it lasts. Wait!

Declaration: *I declare that I am part of a divine plan that cannot fail, and every promise concerning me will manifest in God's perfect time, in Jesus' name.*

Let us pray
1. *Father, I thank You for being a God who finishes what You start in my life, in Jesus' name.*
2. *Father, forgive me for rushing ahead of Your plan and for doubting during seasons of waiting, in Jesus' name.*
3. *O Lord, teach me to value the process and to trust that You are always on time, in Jesus' name.*
4. *Father, help me to focus on pleasing You daily while I wait for Your promises to unfold, in Jesus' name.*
5. *O Lord, strengthen my faith to believe even if the fulfillment comes beyond my lifetime, in Jesus' name.*

Friday 20 February   **THE BEST PRAYER**

Read: Luke 22:39-46

Bible in 1 year: Josh. 22-24
Bible in 2 years: Ex. 2-3

"Father, if you are willing, take this cup from me; yet not my will, but yours be done" (Luke 22:42).

Of all the prayers in Scripture, perhaps none is greater than the one Jesus prayed in Gethsemane: *"Not my will, but Yours be done" (Luke 22:42).* This prayer is the essence of true surrender. It places a believer at the center of God's will, where His power, provision, and purpose flow for a life of impact.

Regrettably, many people approach prayer as a means of persuading God to fulfill their desires. But the best prayer seeks alignment with God's purpose, not persuasion. Jesus could have called legions of angels to avoid the cross, but He chose to surrender. Through that prayer, salvation was secured for the world.

"Surrender" is Greek *'Paradidōmi,' meaning* to hand over, to yield, to entrust fully into another's authority. God wants us to hand over our all to Him and allow Him to direct us in our words, decisions, and actions. This is the pathway to freedom and peace.

To pray *"Lord, cleanse me"* is to ask God to purify our hearts so we can be vessels fit for His use (Psalm 51:10). To pray *"Lord, fill me"* is to invite the Holy Spirit to take control, empowering us for holy living and service (Ephesians 5:18). To pray *"Lord, use me"* is to lay our gifts, resources, and lives on the altar for kingdom purposes (Romans 12:1). These three petitions – cleanse me, fill me, and use me, together reflect the prayer of surrender.

The Bible gives us examples of surrendered lives. Isaiah responded to God's call with, *"Here I am. Send me!" (Isaiah 6:8)*. Paul, after encountering Christ, prayed, *"Lord, what will You have me do?" (Acts 9:6)*. Mary, the mother of Jesus, declared, *"Let it be to me according to Your word" (Luke 1:38)*. Each one of them placed God's will above their own, and through them, His purposes were accomplished.

Beloved, the best prayer is not about eloquence but surrender. When you yield your will to God's will, you step into the safest and most fruitful place a believer can ever be – His perfect plan.

Action: *Quietly ask the Holy Spirit to show you anything or area of your life you have to surrender to God.*

Let us pray
1. *Father, I thank You for the privilege of prayer and for aligning me to Your perfect will, in Jesus' name.*
2. *Lord, cleanse me from every sin and impurity that hinders my walk with You, in Jesus' name.*
3. *Holy Spirit, fill me afresh with Your power and presence, in Jesus' name.*
4. *Lord, use my life as an instrument to glorify You and expand Your kingdom, in Jesus' name.*
5. *Father, help me to embrace Your will above my own desires, no matter the cost, in Jesus' name.*
6. *I declare that my life is surrendered to God; I am cleansed, filled, and used for His glory, in Jesus' name.*

Saturday 21 February   **ROOT IT OUT!**

Read: Proverbs 6:12-19

Bible in 1 year: John 11-13
Bible in 2 years: Ex. 4-5

"Every plant not planted by my heavenly Father will be uprooted" (Matthew 15:13 NLT).

God is a planter of good seed, but the enemy plants destructive weeds to corrupt and choke what God has sown. Jesus said, *"Every plant not planted by my heavenly Father will be uprooted" (Matthew 15:13).* The responsibility of believers is to cooperate with God in identifying and rooting out satanic seeds before they grow into destructive habits.

"*Uproot*" in Greek is '*Ekrizoo*', meaning "To tear out by the roots, to remove completely." True deliverance is not trimming weeds but uprooting them so they never grow back.

Cain is a sobering example. Instead of rejoicing at Abel's favor, he nursed envy and resentment until it matured into murder (Genesis 4:7-8). God warned him to rule over sin before it ruled him, but Cain ignored the warning and reaped tragic consequences. Likewise, when we tolerate weeds of sin: envy, bitterness, lust, or false doctrine, they eventually destroy us.

Scripture shows us examples of these weeds. False doctrine destabilizes faith (1 Timothy 4:1-2). Seeds of discord destroy families and churches (Proverbs 6:16-19). Lust, if unchecked, leads to immorality, as in Amnon's tragedy (2 Samuel 13). Evil spirits may sow seeds of affliction to torment and oppress people (Matthew 17:14-15). Left unchallenged, these weeds grow roots too deep to pull out easily.

But through Christ, we believers have the authority to uproot every plant the Father did not plant. On the cross, Jesus disarmed the powers of darkness (Colossians 2:15). The Holy Spirit exposes hidden weeds in our hearts and empowers us to root them out. Just as a farmer cannot allow weeds to overtake his field, you must act decisively through prayer, repentance, and obedience to God's Word, to destroy every weed in your life.

Action: *Today, examine your heart. What seed has the enemy planted? Root it out now, in Jesus' name!*

Let us pray
1. *Father, thank You for planting good seeds of righteousness in my life, in Jesus' name.*
2. *Lord, expose every hidden weed the enemy has planted in my heart, in Jesus' name.*
3. *I uproot false doctrines and every deception that corrupts my faith, in Jesus' name.*
4. *Father, deliver me from lust, affliction, and every satanic seed designed to destroy me, in Jesus' name.*
5. *I declare: Every evil seed in my life is uprooted. I am fruitful and victorious in Christ, in Jesus' name.*

Sunday 22 February **PEACE BE WITH YOU**

Read: Daniel 3:16-18

Bible in 1 year: John 14-17
Bible in 2 years: Ex. 6-7

"Peace I leave with you; My peace I give you. I do not give to you as the world gives. Do not let your hearts be troubled and do not be afraid" (John 14:27).

God's peace is beyond anything the world can offer. Are you troubled and peaceless because of what you are going through now? God wants to flood your soul with His peace.

Human peace is the absence of conflict or disturbance, but divine peace is the presence of Christ in the midst of conflict. Jesus told His disciples, *"My peace I give you" (John 14:27).* This peace is supernatural – it holds us steady when circumstances are chaotic.

We see this clearly in Scripture. The three Hebrew boys stood before Nebuchadnezzar's fiery furnace without trembling (Daniel 3:16-18). They declared their faith in God even if deliverance didn't come. That calm resolve was not natural, it was the peace of God. Likewise, Peter slept in prison on the eve of his execution (Acts 12:6). How could he rest so soundly? He trusted the Lord's sovereignty. God's peace guarded his heart like an unshakable fortress.

Paul explains the secret: *"Do not be anxious about anything, but in every situation, by prayer and petition, with thanksgiving, present your requests to God. And the peace of God, which transcends all understanding, will guard your hearts and your*

minds in Christ Jesus" (Philippians 4:6–7). The key steps are simple:
1) Inform God about your needs (1 Peter 5:7).
2) Leave the burden with Him – stop carrying it yourself.
3) Begin to thank Him in advance, for gratitude opens the door to His peace.

A brother in the faith once testified of losing a job unexpectedly but, instead of panicking, chose to trust God in prayer and thanksgiving. Within weeks, a better opportunity opened. Peace carried him through the waiting season.

God's peace is your inheritance in Christ. Don't let anxiety eat you up. Hand your worry over to Jesus. He is faithful.

Action: *Get two Bible promises concerning your situation and confess them several times today!*

Let us pray

1. *Father, thank You for giving me the gift of peace through Christ, in Jesus' name.*
2. *Lord, teach me to cast all my cares upon You and trust fully, in Jesus' name.*
3. *Father, deliver me from anxiety and fear that disturb my soul, in Jesus' name.*
4. *O Father, let Your peace rule over my mind, family, and circumstances, in Jesus' name.*
5. *Father, help me live as a witness of peace, pointing others to Christ, in Jesus' name.*

Monday 23 February   **PURIFIED BY GOD**

Read: Matthew 4:1-11

> **Bible in 1 year:** John 18-21
> **Bible in 2 years:** Ex. 8-9

"God will purify many people and make them clean and spotless, while the wicked will continue doing what is wicked. This revelation will remain a riddle to the wicked, but those who are wise will have profound understanding" (Daniel 12:10 TPT).

God's nature is pure, and because He is holy, He cannot look approvingly on evil (Habakkuk 1:13). For this reason, everyone who will serve Him must go through the process of purification.

"*Purify*" in Hebrew is '*Barar*' meaning "To select, cleanse, or refine." Purification is God's process of removing impurities so His people can reflect His holiness. Daniel prophesied that in the last days, many will be purified, refined, and made spotless. *"Many shall be purified, and made white, and tried" (Daniel 12:10).* Purification is not punishment; it is preparation. It is how God shapes vessels fit for His glory.

Even Jesus, though sinless, was tested. He faced the test of appetite when tempted to turn stones into bread (Matthew 4:3-4). He overcame by relying on God's Word, reminding us that our desires must be under the Spirit's control. He faced the test of power when Satan offered Him kingdoms in exchange for worship (Matthew 4:8-10). He chose obedience over ambition. Lastly, He faced the test of pride when told to throw Himself from the temple to prove His identity (Matthew 4:5-7). He refused to seek human validation, trusting the Father instead.

These three tests: appetite, power, and pride, are still the fire through which God purifies us today. The refining is painful at times, but it produces a spotless character that reflects Christ (1 Peter 1:7). Like gold in the furnace, God's people shine brighter after the fire.

As a young believer, fasting and prayer helped me overcome destructive habits I had cultivated before coming to Christ. What once controlled me lost power because God was purifying my desires. God is still purifying and refining hearts today.

Do you want to be used by God? He must purify you first (2 Timothy 2:21). Let the Spirit refine you. What God purifies, He also empowers.

Action: *Are you struggling with a bad habit? Confess it to your pastor. Fast and pray for deliverance.*

Let us pray
1. *Father, thank You for Your refining fire that prepares me for Your service, in Jesus' name.*
2. *Lord, purge my heart from hidden sins and secret faults, in Jesus' name.*
3. *Father, deliver me from the grip of uncontrolled appetites and desires, in Jesus' name.*
4. *O Lord, keep me from chasing after power and fame outside Your will, in Jesus' name.*
5. *Father, break every root of pride in me; clothe me with humility and Christ-like character, in Jesus' name.*

6. *I declare: I am purified by God, refined as gold, and set apart for His glory, in Jesus' name.*

Prophetic Prayers of the Week
1. **"I will instruct you and teach you." (Psalm 32:8)** *God will lead me into His perfect will today, in Jesus' name.*
2. **"A diligent man will stand before kings." (Proverbs 22:29)** *I will rise into excellence and influence my generation, in Jesus' name.*
3. **No weapon formed against you shall prosper." (Isaiah 54:17)** *Every attack against me this week will fail woefully, in Jesus' name.*

Tuesday 24 February **IS SOMEONE TRYING TO BRING YOU DOWN?**

Read: Daniel 6:1-24

> **Bible in 1 year:** 1 Kings 1-4
> **Bible in 2 years:** Ex. 10-11

"Do you see a man skilled in his work? He will stand before kings; he will not stand before obscure men" (Proverbs 22:29).

While some are excited by your promotion, others are infuriated. But never forget that God protects the ones He has promoted. Psalm 121:3 says, *"He will not let you fall..."*

Daniel's rise to prominence stirred envy among his colleagues. His extraordinary spirit and integrity made him a target for plots and manipulation. Yet no matter how they schemed, they could not find fault in him, except in matters concerning his faith. This reveals an important truth: when God's favor lifts you, opposition will come, but INTEGRITY and FAITHFULNESS will preserve you.

Why did Daniel overcome? First, he distinguished himself by excellence. Mediocrity never glorifies God, but a life of diligence does (Colossians 3:23). Second, he was free from negligence and corruption. While others compromised, Daniel maintained integrity. Third, he was consistent in his devotion to God. Even when praying put his life at risk, he refused to abandon his spiritual discipline (Daniel 6:10).

Many times, colleagues or peers try to bring others down out of jealousy or insecurity. Instead of fighting back with the same weapons, believers are called to respond with godly character. Proverbs 22:29 says, *"Do you see a man skilled in his work? He will stand before kings; he will not stand before obscure men."* When you walk in integrity, God Himself defends and promotes you.

A sister in the faith was being falsely accused at work. Instead of retaliating, she kept her faith and served diligently. Months later, her accusers were exposed, and she was promoted. Her integrity outlasted their schemes.

Friend, is someone trying to bring you down? Remember: God's favor is greater than their plots. Live above reproach, remain faithful to God, and trust Him to vindicate you.

Action: *Identify one way you want to improve the quality of your work. Pray and do it!*

Let us pray

1. *Father, thank You for the example of Daniel's integrity and faithfulness, in Jesus' name.*
2. *Lord, give me an excellent spirit that distinguishes me in every area of life, in Jesus' name.*
3. *Father, deliver me from negligence, corruption, and compromise, in Jesus' name.*
4. *O LORD, protect me from envy, lies, and manipulations at work or ministry, in Jesus' name.*
5. *I declare: No plot against me shall stand – God's favor will lift me higher, in Jesus' name.*

Wednesday 25 February — **YOUR NAME SHOULD NOT STOP YOU**

Read: Daniel 1:3-16

Bible in 1 year: 1 Kings 5-8
Bible in 2 years: Ex. 12

"Therefore, if anyone is in Christ, he is a new creation. The old has passed away; behold, the new has come" (2 Corinthians 5:17).

Through the new birth, you have been born into God's family. As God's legitimate child, you have a new name. Search for your new name in the Bible. Whatever name Satan and the world are trying to impose on you has no effect. Don't submit to it!

When Daniel and his friends were taken into Babylon, the first attack on their destiny was identity. The chief official gave them new Babylonian names connected to foreign gods. Daniel was called Belteshazzar (linked to Bel, a pagan deity); Hananiah was called Shadrach; Mishael became Meshach; and Azariah was renamed Abednego. This strategy was meant to strip them of their covenant identity and assimilate them into Babylonian culture.

But while their names were changed, their dedication to God remained unshaken. Daniel *"Determined not to defile himself"* (v.8). Names imposed by others, whether labels of failure, limitation, or ridicule, cannot stop a person whose heart is consecrated to God. In Christ, you carry a new identity: *"If anyone is in Christ, he is a new creation"* (2 Corinthians 5:17).

Maybe, like Jabez, the name given to you at birth does not align with your destiny. Jabez, whose name meant "Sorrow," prayed, and God transformed his story (1 Chronicles 4:9-10). What matters most is not what people call you, but the God you serve and the focus you maintain. Your radical consecration will set you apart for glorious things.

I know a successful brother who was once ridiculed as a school failure. He held firmly to God's promises. Today, the same people who mocked him are celebrating his success after God elevated him professionally. His dedication outweighed the labels.

Daniel shows us that names may be imposed, but they don't define destiny. Stay faithful, keep your consecration, and God will make your true identity shine.

Action: *Is there a wrong name or identity Satan is trying to impose on you? Identify and reject it firmly!*

Let us pray

1. *Father, thank You for giving me a new identity in Christ, in Jesus' name.*
2. *Lord, silence every wrong label or name spoken over my life, in Jesus' name.*
3. *Father, deliver me from the fear of human opinions and false identities, in Jesus' name.*
4. *Father, help me walk in radical consecration and refuse defilement, in Jesus' name.*
5. *O Father, let my true destiny and calling in Christ shine above every false name, in Jesus' name.*
6. *I declare: No name given by man can stop me – I walk in my God-given identity and destiny, in Jesus' name.*

Thursday 26 February   **SOURCE OF FAMILY STRENGTH**

Read: Luke 22:39-46

Bible in 1 year: 1 Kings 9-12
Bible in 2 years: Ex. 13-14

"Watch and pray so that you will not fall into temptation. The spirit is willing, but the flesh is weak" (Matthew 26:41 NIV).

Do you know that effective prayer is the hidden engine of an unbreakable family? Jesus did not merely instruct His disciples about prayer; He demonstrated it. On the night of His betrayal, He entered the Garden of Gethsemane and prayed with such intensity that His sweat became like drops of blood (Luke 22:44). That depth of prayer gave Him strength to face the cross and complete His mission.

    Your family can draw tremendous power from her prayer altar. Sadly, families that neglect the prayer altar struggle under demonic oppressions and manipulations. I have witnessed several families rise as they set up prayer altars and begin to pray fervently. In 1995, our household raised a prophetic altar where we gathered to intercede for healing, direction, and breakthrough. Over the years, we witnessed God's hand bringing restoration, provision, and miracles. That altar became the center of unity and transformation in our family, proving that prayer is more than words; it is the meeting place with God where destinies are shaped.

When Jesus warned His disciples, *"Watch and pray so that you will not fall into temptation" (Matthew 26:41)*, He revealed that prayer shields us from weakness. Friend, temptation, conflict, and pressure will come, but your prayer will provide endurance, discernment, and victory. Without effective prayer, even your strongest intentions will collapse under pressure. So, don't neglect your family prayer altar for any reason.

Friend, do you have a family altar? If not, consider bringing your family together to create a vibrant prayer altar. Nowadays, raising a family altar is easy. It can be in your sitting room, around a table, through phone calls, or virtual gatherings. The method may change, but the principle is timeless. Let your children hear your voice as you pray in the storm and sing in the valley. Teach them that prayer is not a last resort but the first line of defense.

A family that prays together is not easily broken. They remain united, strong, and victorious, carrying God's presence into every season of life.

Action: *Raise a family prayer altar within the next 7 days if you don't have one!*

Let us pray

1. *Father, thank You for the gift of prayer that keeps our family close to You and to one another, in Jesus' name.*
2. *Holy Spirit, ignite a fresh passion for prayer in every member of my household, in Jesus' name.*
3. *Father, let our family altar be filled with Your presence, power, and glory, in Jesus' name.*
4. *Father, uproot every spirit of distraction, laziness, and apathy that weakens our prayer life, in Jesus' name.*

5. Father, raise watchmen and intercessors among our children and family members, in Jesus' name.
6. I declare that God's fire will never go out on my family altar, in Jesus' name!

Friday 27 February   **HE WILL CARRY YOU**

Read: Isaiah 46:3-4

Bible in 1 year: 1 Kings 13-15
Bible in 2 years: Ex. 15-16

"The eternal God is your dwelling place, and underneath are the everlasting arms" (Deuteronomy 33:27).

Life often brings moments when strength fails, dreams collapse, and pain overwhelms us. Like Derek Redmond in the 1992 Olympics, we may start strong but suddenly fall. Yet Isaiah 46:4 reminds us of a powerful truth: the God who made us also carries us. He doesn't abandon us in weakness. He bears us up in His everlasting arms. This is also seen in Deuteronomy 33:27: *"The eternal God is your dwelling place, and underneath are the everlasting arms."*

Israel often struggled with burdens, idols, and enemies. But God declared that, unlike the lifeless gods of Babylon, who had to be carried, He Himself would carry His people. This is the difference between religion and relationship. We do not carry God; He carries us. Jesus reaffirmed this when He said, *"Come to Me, all you who are weary and burdened, and I will give you rest" (Matthew 11:28).*

When Paul was overwhelmed, he discovered this truth: *"My grace is sufficient for you, for My power is made perfect in weakness"* (2 Corinthians 12:9). God's strength is revealed most clearly when we can no longer walk on our own.

Jim Redmond stepped in to help his son finish the 400-meter race after he tore his hamstring during the 1992 Barcelona Olympics. The father stepping onto the track to carry his son mirrors how our heavenly Father steps into our brokenness. He does not watch from a distance but runs to us, embraces us, and says, *"We will finish this together."*

Are you weary, burdened, or broken today? The same God who formed you is committed to sustaining you. He will not only carry you through pain but also ensure you finish the race of faith. You will make it in Jesus' name!

Declaration: Declare this throughout today: *"I am not alone. God's hand will carry me through this challenge, in Jesus' name!*

Let us pray

1. *Father, thank You for carrying me in times of weakness and sustaining me daily, in Jesus' name.*
2. *Lord, lift me when I fall and bear me through the challenges of life, in Jesus' name.*
3. *Father, break the burden of self-reliance and teach me to lean wholly on You, in Jesus' name.*
4. *Father, strengthen me to trust You when I feel too weak to move forward, in Jesus' name.*
5. *Father, carry my family, church, and nation through every storm into Your purpose this year, in Jesus' name.*

Saturday 28 February   **FAILURE IS NOT AN OPTION**

Read: Philippians 3:12-16

Bible in 1 year: 1 Kings 16-19
Bible in 2 years: (Catch-up)

"But one thing I do: Forgetting what is behind and straining toward what is ahead, I press on toward the goal to win the prize for which God has called me heavenward in Christ Jesus" (Philippians 3:13-14).

Do you know that every breakthrough begins with a decision: *FAILURE IS NOT AN OPTION?* Many people quit too soon because they secretly leave themselves an escape route. The Israelites turned back in their hearts toward Egypt whenever the wilderness grew tough (Acts 7:39). They never entered God's best because they allowed the thought of quitting in their minds.

Paul's words in Philippians 3 show us the mindset of a winner. He refused to be defined by past setbacks and resolved to press on toward the heavenly calling. Likewise, Jesus warned in Luke 9:62 that *"No one who puts a hand to the plow and looks back is fit for service in the kingdom of God."* To walk with God is to embrace perseverance – refusing to retreat even when trials seem unbearable.

"Press on" in Greek is *'Dioko'*, meaning "To pursue with determination, to run after, to never give up." This is the mentality you need to seek and serve God till the end.

Marriage provides a vivid picture. Many couples enter with an unspoken option of quitting. When storms come, this mindset weakens their resolve. But those who remove "Divorce" from their vocabulary fight through challenges, grow in love, and build lasting legacies. The same principle applies to ministry, business, and faith.

When we got married in 1999, we agreed on this: "My wife will never say, 'I will quit,' and that I should never tell her, 'Leave this house.'" More than twenty-five years later, we are enjoying our marriage, not enduring it. The door called "QUIT" was closed, and the key was thrown away.

The Christian journey requires a similar resolve. With Christ living in us, quitting is not an option. Victory belongs to those who decide to persevere.

Action: *Are you thinking of quitting your marriage or an assignment God has given you? Decide not to quit and ask God for grace.*

Let us pray
1. *Father, thank You for giving me the strength to persevere in Christ, in Jesus' name.*
2. *Lord, remove every mindset of quitting from my heart, in Jesus' name.*
3. *Father, strengthen me to press on toward Your calling, no matter the challenges, in Jesus' name.*
4. *Father, visit those who are overwhelmed and want to quit marriage or ministry, and renew them, in Jesus' name.*
5. *Father, help me fix my eyes on the prize and not on present difficulties, in Jesus' name.*
6. *I declare: Failure is not an option; I will press on to victory through Christ, in Jesus' name.*

WHAT YOUR SUPPORT WILL DO

It is very clear through the numerous miracles, breakthroughs and transformation of lives that God has chosen to use this ministry to stir a revival among His people in Cameroon and beyond. I received the call alone but I cannot execute it alone. You have a unique role to play in this divine project. Join us as we take the Gospel to every corner of Cameroon and beyond.

We want to start placing copies of this book in hotels, hospitals, schools and homes, to touch the lives of people with the gospel of Jesus Christ. Just as you have been blessed by this book, they too will be mightily blessed.

TESTIMONY

Every month, hundreds of copies of this Prayer Storm Daily Prayer Guide are distributed freely, thanks to the kind gesture of our partners. May God bless all of you who faithfully sponsor this outreach through your financial seed. You too can sponsor 10, 25, 50, 100 or even more copies to be printed and distributed charge-free to those who are hungry for the word.

Call the numbers: (237) 699.90.26.18 or 674.49.58.95 send an email to voiceofrevivalcameroon@yahoo.com.

If you want to become a distributor of our literature, contact us directly and we will give you the directives on how to do so.

WHERE TO BUY THIS PRAYER GUIDE

CRN Centres
- **Yaounde:** *Prayer Storm Headquarters:* 1st Floor Storey Building at Entrée Lycée de Tsinga village on the edge of the main road. **Contact:** 681.72.24.04/ 696.56.58.64
- **Bamenda:** Revival Christian Book Center, **Cow Street**: 675.14.04.50/ 694.20.04.51
- **Douala/PK 8:** All American Depot opposite Lycée **Cité des Palmiers**: 678.04.11.41/ 696.90.76.09/ 670.34.42.32

Adamawa
- **Banyo:** FGM: 677.92.05.98/ 674.64.71.31
- **Meinganga:** EEL: 699.65.02.67/ 652.70.40.68
- **Ngaoundere:** EEC Mont des Oliviers: 674.14.20.51, EEL: 690.06.37.14
- **Tibati:** EEC: 681.01.33.34

Centre
- **Eseka:** FGM: 675.07.56.24
- **Mbalmayo:** EEC: 675.12.86.85/
- **Mfou:** FGM: 677.36.43.28
- **Monatelé:** FGM: 677.58.42.99
- **Yaounde:** EEC **Biyem-assi**: 675.61.86.00/ 677.49.95.83/ 691.26.18.08, EEC **Nlongkak**: 677.56.41.09, EEC **Nouvelle Alliance**: 670.80.56.93, FGM **Biyem-assi**: 675.14.72.70, FGM **Etoug-Ebé**: 671.47.75.78/ 673.50.42.33, Galaxy Computers, Châteaux **Ngoa-Ekelle**: 670.52.75.26, **Yaounde:** Librairie Chrétienne Les Champions op. Total Caveau, **Mvog-Ada**: 675.51.02.86, **LC Maison de la Grâce**, Montée Jouvence op. Olympia: 675.38.46.96, **LC Maison de la Bénédiction**, Marché

Nsam: 691.64.47.84, **LC la Rhema**, Marché Essos, Terminus: 679.39.37.42, **LC Maison du Salut**, Pharmacie du Soleil, Carrefour MEEC: 674.85.16.33/ 699.33.85.11, **LC Livre de Vie**, Mini ferme: 675.00.45.60, **LC Bethesda**, Tsinga: 679.97.06.26, **Overcomers Christian Bookshop**, op. Djongolo Hospital, EtoaMeki: 677.16.46.20, **Mount Zion Christian Bookshop**, op. SONEL TKC: 663.25.86.23 / 675.21.94.35, **Tongolo**: 675.62.86.00, **Olembe**: 651.63.52.34, **DGI-Carrefour Abbia** 652.22.22.49, **Messassi**: 675.24.70.73, **Nkozoa**: 670.29.50.18, **Essos**: 677.53.94.52, **Odzja**: 679.97.47.08, **Etoug-Ebé**: 675.37.18.11, **Mimboman**: 699.90.52.84, **Poste Centrale**: 650.70.08.07, **Emombo**: 699.90.52.84, **Lycée Emana**: 677.86.23.14

East

- **Batouri:** FGM: 664.86.41.80
- **Bertoua:** CBC, **quartier Ngaikada** ou **Aprilé centrale** sous-préfecture: 678.00.63.20/ 694.25.69.20, Collège Bilingue de l'Orient, entrée Hôpital Régionale, **quartier Italy**: 670.56.81.49, FGM, **Nkolbikon**: 696.57.95.43, 677.65.46.76, FGM, **Tigaza**: 674.15.13.18
- **Yokadouma:** FGM: 673.16.24.95/ 696.51.73.70

Far-North

- **Maroua:** Église Missionnaire du Réveil (EMIR) **Baoliwop**: 694.43.33.63, FGM **Harde**: 675.33.12.27, Roman Catholic Church: 673.15.19.76
- **Yagoua:** FGM: 675.691.869

Littoral

Douala: Dakar: La Gloire Phone, immeuble X Tigi, Commissariat 11e: 697.60.57.85, **Kotto:** Behind Neptune fuel station, **Bloc M:** 677.68.18.52, **Bonaberi:** 677.89.87.46, **Akwa:** 691.04.14.59/ 677.91.29.45, **Logpom:** 677.68.18.52/ 651.78.57.30, **Carrefour Lycée de Maképé:** 698.09.42.63, **PK 12 (Marché):** 677.91.29.45/ 696.13.99.26, **Texaco-Nkoulouluon:** 675.18.79.85/695112610 691.04.14.59, **Terminus Saint Michel :** 675187985, La Gloire Phone, Maison X. Tigi, **Carrefour entrée Bille:** 678.19.90.85, **PK 21:** 670.79.05.40/ 691.04.14.59, **Bonanjo:** 691.04.14.59, 677061705 691.04.14.59, **Ange Raphael ESSEC:** 694.26.12.28/ 677.91.29.45, 698360441, **Bonamoussadi Maetur:** 694.26.12.28/ 677.91.29.45, **Village:** 670.79.05.40/ 691.04.14.5, Sure Foundation **Bonabéri:** Ancienne route op. Lycée de Bonaberi Winners Chapel: 671.403.761

- **Nkongsamba:** FGM: 676.40.90.55
- **Melong - GCEPAL:** Tel: 677.80.16.45

North

- **Garoua:** FGM: 678.67.04.22/ 699.91.91.65

North-West

- **Bamenda:** Bamenda Main Market, **Shed 15**: 679.45.11.88, Carmel Cooperative Credit Union (CarCCUL), **Sonac Street**/Tél: 651.04.21.27, FGM NW1 Area office, opposite Garanti Express: 679.46.63.31, FGM, **Cow Street**: 677.21.97.22, FGM, **Mbomassa**: 683.40.40.88, Omega Fire Ministry, **Foncha junction**: 677.93.19.98, ACADI head office, **Wakiki junction**: 672.82.77.84, SUMAN Christian Book Center, **Sonac Street**: 675.72.91.32/ 665.49.98.48, Victory Computers, Food

market, **Fishpond hill**: 677.64.19.54, Wailing Women: 696.00.35.07/ 674.57.36.76
- **Batibo:** FGM: 677.31.25.45
- **Njinikom/Mbingo:** BERUDA: 677.60.14.07
- **Jakiri:** FGM, **Nkar**: 677.73.82.91
- **Kumbo:** FGM: 675.72.91.32
- **Mbengwi:** FGM: 677.33.73.86
- **Ndop:** Bruno Bijouterie, Central park: 674.97.59.34
- **Wum:** FGM Central Town: 677.64.32.56, PCC Kesu: 677.13.83.51

<u>West</u>
- **Bafang:** FGM, **Bafang**: 655.00.25.57
- **Bafia:** FGM: 675.21.92.95/ 695.54.96.14
- **Bafoussam:** Alliance biblique du Cameroun, **Tamdja**, SOREPCO: 699.74.79.10, Radio Bonne Nouvelle: 699.93.09.32, Librairie chrétienne du **Camp** oignon: 699.51.47.25, LC PAROLE DE VIE, **gare routière de** Ndiangdam: 699.75.50.99, Dépôt RAYON AMBIANCE **marché A**: 699.42.78.47, EEC **Tamdja**: 696.14.90.16, EEC **Kamkop**: 699.44.03.59, EEC **Plateau**: 696.17.54.23, EEC **Toket**: 695.56.43.61, EEC **SOCADA**: 697.85.65.65, EEC **Tyo-Baleng**: 670.89.70.52, EEC **Kouogouo**: 675.42.27.86, EEC **Diangdam**: 698.35.20.37, FGM **Kamkop**: 653.83.11.80, Faith Bible Church: 683.94.01.21
- **Baham:** FGM: 677.47.55.79
- **Bandjoun:** FGM: 676.41.49.09
- **Bangangte:** EEC **Banekane**: 677.86.47.68
- **Banyo:** FGM: 677.92.05.98/ 674.64.71.31
- **Dschang:** FGM: 675.18.79.85/ 656.20.07.02, FGM **Minmeto**: 681.08.78.37/ 655.01.81.09

- **Foumban:** Décoration Splendeur, **CAMOCO**/Tel.: 677.79.30.83/ 694.85.09.25
- **Kombou:** EEC: 675.81.36.07
- **Mbouda:** FGM: 696.10.41.33/ 676.36.18.11, Cyber Café Pressing near Espace Saint Pierre du Fossie, op. Party House: 675.00.91.15, EEC **Mbouda Centre**: 695.61.97.79

South
- **Ebolowa:** FGM: 677.66.00.19/ 671.90.97.22
- **Kribi:** Carrefour Django: 675.957.912
- **Kye-Ossi:** FGM: 678.78.00.90/ 699.95.96.99

South-West
- **Buea:** FGM **Molyko**: 677.86.47.68, Molyko, near Express Union, **Check Point**: 675.06.37.78,
- **Ekona:** FGM: 675.84.26.91
- **Kumba:** Caisse Populaire Coopérative Carmel (CarCCUL), **Sonac Street**: 675.45.12.21, Glorious Christian Book Center, **Sonac Street**: 677.62.58.49
- **Lebialem:** FGM de **Talung**, Bamumbu – Wabane: 670.466.121
- **Limbe:** Librairie Amen, **New town**: 677.16.51.62, FGM **Mawoh**: 675.78.94.19, FGM **Cow Fence**: 675.73.20.02
- **Misaje:** Kingdom Restoration Parish (KRP) **opposite the hospital**: 679.33.66.53
- **Mutengene:** FGM: 675.36.36.84
- **Muyuka:** FGM: 673.428.985, Royal Priesthood Nursery and Primary School: 677.72.76.80
- **Tiko:** FGM: 654.88.75.57, 674.47.34.36
- **Tombel:** Baptist Church Waterfall: 677.92.33.58

ABROAD:

- **N'Djamena (Chad):** Evang. Kaltouma Aguidi: (235) 95.01.99.92
- **Libreville (Gabon):** Rev. Petipa Flaubert: (241) 05.31.27.39

Pay for your book orders (DISTRIBUTORS ONLY) at:
EcoBank, Acc. No: 0200212620638901 **or** ORANGE Mobile Money, Acc. No: 696880058
Info lines: (237) 677436964, 675686005, 673571953, 679465717;
crnprayerstorm@gmail.com,
prayerstorm@christianrestorationnetwork.org,
www.christianrestorationnetwork.org

Send Financial Support to: ECOBANK Bamenda Acc. No: 0040812604565101 **or** Carmel Cooperative Credit Union Ltd. Bamenda Acc. No: 261 **or** ORANGE Mobile Money: 699902618 **or** MTN Mobile Money: 674495895.

PUBLICATIONS BY CHRISTIAN RESTORATION NETWORK (CRN/PRAYER STORM)

1- Prayer Storm Daily Prayer Guide (monthly devotional)
2- Power Must Change Hands Vol.1: Dealing with Evil Foundations
3- Power Must Change Hands Vol.2: Pursue Overtake and Recover All
4- Power Must Change Hands Vol.3: Jesus Christ Must Reign
5- Power Must Change Hands Vol.4: Arise and Shine
6- Power Must Change Hands Vol.5: Family Restoration 1
7- Power Must Change Hands Vol.6: Family Restoration 2
8- Power Must Change Hands Vol.7: Raise an Altar
9- Power Must Change Hands Vol.8: Commanding Total Victory
10- Power Must Change Hands Vol.9: Enjoying Your Freedom in Christ
11- Power Must Change Hands Vol.10: Supernatural Breakthrough
12- Festival of Fire Series No.1: Let the Fire Fall
13- Festival of Fire Series No.2: Anointed Vessels
14- Festival of Fire Series No.3: God's Agent of Revival
15- Festival of Fire Series No.4: Raising Altars of Restoration
16- Festival of Fire Series No.5: Foundations of a Blessed Family
17- Dominion
18- Divine Overflow
19- Unbreakable

20- Higher Heights
21- Arresting Family Destroyers 1
22- Arresting Family Destroyers 2
23- Praying Like Jesus
24- Conquering the Giant Called Poverty
25- Generous Living
26- Bind the Strongman
27- Personal and Family Deliverance
28- A Difference by Fire
29- Your Time for Divine Expansion
30- Jesus Our Jubilee
31- The Choice of a Friend
32- Christians and Politics
33- A Dynamic Prayer Life
34- Restoring Broken Foundations

NB: Our publications are in English and French.

For copies, contact your local books store or direct your request to:

Prayer Storm Team
P.O. Box 5018 Nkwen, Bamenda
Tel.: (237) 679465717 or 675686005 or 677436964
crnprayerstorm@gmail.com
prayerstorm@christianrestorationnetwork.org

Prayer Storm Online Store:

With MTN or Orange Mobile Money *(for those in Cameroon)* and E-Wallet *(for those abroad)*, you can easily obtain the electronic version of this book and other CRN publications via **www.amazon.com** or via **www.amazon.com** at

https://shorturl.at/pqxyT or
www.christianrestorationnetwork.org/our-bookstore.
https://goo.gl/ktf3rT

Contact (237) 679.46.57.17 or
prayerstorm@christianrestorationnetwork.org